A PLACE IN PROVENCE

To Betty

With Best Wishes

Jane French.

Jane French

A PLACE IN PROVENCE

To Richard, Katharine and Alison

CONTENTS

CHAPTER ONE

ANTICIPATION

'Provence! We're going for a whole year to Aix-en-Provence!' Richard was euphoric, dancing me around the kitchen, our two infant daughters, four year old Katharine and two year old Alison, watching saucer-eyed from the doorway.

'But we've got no money,' I laughed, out of breath. 'How on earth can we afford to go to Provence?'

The girls' eyes moved from me to their father.

'Oh – we'll think of something,' said Richard with a breezy sweep of his arm, as if brushing away all obstacles. 'But you will all come with me, I promise,' and laughing with pleasure at the prospect, he picked up his daughters, one by one and, holding them high in the air, whizzed them too around the kitchen, much to their delight.

He was nearing the end of the spring term of his first year as a mature student of Linguistics at York University, for which one of the main attractions had been the 'year abroad' to study French. Richard had already lived and worked abroad for quite a few years before I met him, first of all in Hong Kong in business, and then in the Army. Indeed, it was during his tour in Libya as an officer with the British Army that we had first met. I was working for the Foreign Office and planning to go on travelling for as long as I possibly could, my one desire being to see as much of the world as possible. Then Richard came along with much the same ambition and before I knew what was happening we were married and posted, unwillingly, back to the U.K.

Richard promised me then that one day we would go on our travels again, but for the next few years I was too busy bringing up my two baby daughters to think about anything else. Meantime, Richard had left the Army and was now studying for a degree in preparation for a new career in teaching.

Just now he was leafing through an atlas, looking for the clearest map of France. He spread the map out on the table in front of three pairs of eager eyes as he explained.

'When Professor le Page told us this morning that the students going to France next year had a choice between Vincennes University in Paris, Lyons, or the University of Aix-Marseilles and that the lists were up on the Common Room notice board, I didn't waste a second. I went straight down and signed up for Aix. I hope you agree, ' Richard asked me rather anxiously 'but you see, I had to get my name down quickly or we might have been sent wherever they had space for me, and I certainly don't want you and the girls to have to live in a big city like Paris or Lyons'.

'But Marseilles is a big city too, and a port,' I replied, 'and I don't altogether like the sound of it.'

'Yes, but we'll be going to the Aix campus, and Aix is a beautiful little town. Look, here it is, right in the heart of Provence.' The girls scrambled to get a look, but were not very impressed, obviously expecting more than just a dot on the map.

But for me, one look at the map was enough. A beautiful little town in the heart of Provence. There was no further doubt in my mind.

'Aix-en-Provence... Oh yes, I could certainly live there. I've heard of it before. I must find out more about it, though. I'll go to the Library.'

Richard was grinning with relief. 'Thank heaven,' he sighed. 'I was pretty sure you'd agree.'

Aix was the obvious choice for us. Richard, born in a city, had always hated city life and although I as a country girl found cities exciting, I was quite happy to live in a smaller town, especially with two small children and, as far as I was concerned, if the whole family really could go with him, then Provence would be a dream come true.

So we sat down and tried to work out how we were going to find enough money to finance our year in France.

It was immediately clear that on the student's grant of less than one thousand pounds a year we would not be able to afford to rent a house or flat in Aix, never mind provide food and all the other necessities of life for a family of four. It was difficult enough to make ends meet in York, where we owned, or rather had a mortgage on our own house, and where I had found a part-time job to help our finances. In France, however, it would be impossible for me, with 'O' Level French, or what I remembered of it, to find work. Anyway, I would have to look after the children.

So where would we live? Over the following days and weeks we devoted much thought and discussion to this problem, and the solution that we came up with seemed to meet with the agreement of every one of us, including the girls.

As a family, we had already taken several camping holidays in Scotland and Ireland, and we knew there was an excellent network of campsites throughout France. While we usually camped in our ancient blue frame tent, once or twice we had stayed in a caravan belonging to relatives. There was something very alluring about caravan life, especially for little girls who enjoyed playing dolls' house. I began to read them excerpts from 'Wind in the Willows' and now one of their favourite bedtime stories was the story of Toad's yellow caravan. Then they would look at the picture of Toad sitting at the front of his horse-drawn caravan with the road winding into the distance, and hug themselves with sheer delight. The lure of the open road was irresistible. Toad had felt it, the girls felt it, and so did we.

But our caravan would not be for the journey alone. With a mixture of optimism and ignorance we imagined that the weather in the South of France would be mild enough for us to live in a caravan in Provence throughout the year. We decided that what we needed to do, therefore, was to buy a suitable caravan and our travel and accommodation problems for the year in France would be solved.

We set about looking for a suitable caravan without delay, but quickly realised that it was not going to be easy. With one or two exceptions, the caravans we saw were very expensive and in the end it was a matter of what we could afford that determined our choice in the matter. Finally, early that summer, we answered an advertisement in the local paper and bought a small second hand caravan from a private seller. With great excitement we towed it back home, where it stood parked by the side of the house until my mother, who was visiting us a few weeks later, saw what we had bought, and shook her head.

'How on earth are you going to live in that little caravan for a year?' she asked incredulously. We explained that it was the best we could afford, and after some discussion she offered to lend us whatever we needed to buy a bigger, more modern caravan.

We eventually found a much more suitable caravan, reasonably modern and strongly built, with enough space for the children to have a curtained off double bed at one end, separated from the rest of the living area. In the middle of the caravan was the cooking area and cupboards, and at the opposite end was a table with two cushioned benches, which transformed into a double bed for Richard and me. Where the previous caravan had quite small windows, this one had two large windows, one at each end and two windows at each side of the caravan. The curtains were a cheerful tomato-red cotton, slightly faded from the sun, and I fixed up a heavy curtain in a similar shade of pinkish-red to act as a partition, closing off the girls' 'bedroom'.

The girls were bursting with excitement when we towed the new caravan back home, and they were the envy of all their friends as Katharine, shadowed by Alison, proudly showed them around their home-to-be in France.

Richard meantime had made enquiries at the University and had offered our house for letting during our absence, preferably to University staff. In this way he quickly found a tenant in the person of a visiting Professor of Economics, from Montreal University, who needed accommodation in

York for the 1970/71 academic year, the same period we would be in France.

Soon after his arrival in York, sometime in July, we invited the Professor to come for lunch so that he could look over the house. Professor Bulmer proved to be quite a young man, and was delighted with our modern three-bedroomed house and garden in a small estate in the quiet village of Wilberfoss, eight miles from York University. After lunch, we showed him around the house, answering his questions and explaining to him how to operate the washing machine, the immersion heater and other electrical gadgets.

We proposed to ask about twenty pounds per month rent – the same amount that we paid to our Building Society for the Mortgage. This sum was so modest that he couldn't quite believe it. He would have had to pay several times that amount in Canada, he told us, and he offered to pay us at least twice what we asked.

We should have accepted this offer, of course, but as landlords we were pretty naive and ignorant of what lay ahead of us. The original rent seemed fair to us, so that was agreed. When we asked the Professor if there was anything else he wanted to know, he looked at our open fireplace, admitted that he had never lit a fire in his life and asked us to show him how to do it.

We found it very amusing that this man, who came from Canada, a country which above all others we associated with the outdoor life, who had reached the peak of knowledge in his particular field of study, the economics of the Common Market, could not perform the most basic survival task of all – lighting a fire. Had he never been in the Boy Scouts? Had he never read Jack London's gripping short story of survival in the Canadian wilderness, 'To light a fire'? Had he never lit a campfire? He shook his head in shame. He had lived all his life in centrally heated apartments and houses in his Canadian city, where open fires in houses were virtually unknown.

And so we taught the Professor of Economics of

Montreal University something that day which no one had ever taught him before – how to light a fire. When we asked him to do it himself, he fumbled nervously with paper, sticks and matches as though he were handling dynamite, but when he succeeded in producing a flame and watched it grow into a fire, he was as proud as any small boy who had performed this elemental task for the first time.

The marathon of packing the caravan began in earnest now, and in the spaces under the seats we stowed plastic bags containing all the sheets, towels and clothes we thought we would need throughout the seasons until the following summer. We already had sleeping bags, but added a few extra rugs, just in case they were needed. All the usual pots and pans, crockery and cutlery was packed into the kitchen cupboards and in any remaining space we stashed away as much dried and tinned food as we could fit in for the journey.

We bought water containers, torches, camping gaz, everything that we could imagine would be necessary for survival on our journey and in the months of gypsy living that stretched ahead. Richard spent happy hours plotting our route south to Aix with the help of a Michelin Guide and a large-scale map of France.

The girls had collected together their favourite books and I caught them stowing in the caravan an army of dolls and toys which would have filled the caravan on their own, never mind the rest of us. Very unwillingly they were persuaded to take only those they really needed.

We ourselves had a similar problem with books. Richard obviously had to bring all those he needed for his studies, which left me very little space for more than one or two books to read on the journey. Later on I would regret having so little reading matter, as English novels were not easy to find in rural France.

At last we were ready. The caravan was packed to the gills and hitched behind our car, a navy blue Ford Cortina Estate, which our local Garage had fitted with a reconditioned engine. Sam Jackson, our trusty Mechanic, assured us the car was as good as new, and would take us to Kingdom Come and back. We reminded him that we just wanted it to take us to France!

I made sure that the girls had plenty of colouring books and toys to keep them from getting bored on the long cramped journey to Provence. There was plenty of room in the back of the car for the girls to lie down and sleep on the journey if they were drowsy, although they couldn't understand why they couldn't travel in the caravan itself.

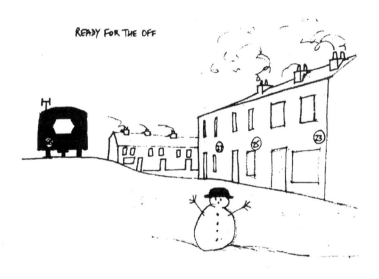

READY FOR THE OFF

We explained that it was dangerous, and in any case against the law, so they had to be content with that. Many years later in northern France we witnessed a fast-moving caravan disintegrate and break into a thousand pieces, just because it swayed slightly as it was towed past some traffic and touched a lorry on the inside lane. That was terrifying spectacle, even though no one was hurt

The summer holidays passed quite quickly and suddenly it was September, and our long wait was over. The day of our departure dawned. The plan was to leave as soon as possible after breakfast, but we were still not ready to go by midday. By then I was exhausted with the effort not only of all the packing but of the last minute clearing up in the house, making it ready for Professor Bulmer to move in immediately. When lunchtime came everyone was hungry, but I put my foot down, and turned them out of my pristine kitchen.

'There's no way that I'm going to start cooking again, making more washing up and having to clear up yet again. You'll just have to wait until we get going. After all, we can eat whenever we like on the road.' Fortunately, this idea appealed to the children, and they kept hunger at bay with a banana until at last all was ready.

As we closed the front door of our house, took our places in the car, and slowly moved away with our caravan home behind us, the neighbours in our little housing estate surprised us by coming out of their houses, calling 'Bon Voyage' and waving us off cheerfully, even though we knew that some of them thought us quite mad, while others were more than a little envious of our chance to get away and live a completely different life for a whole year.

Chapter Two

EN ROUTE

After about ten minutes' driving we pulled off the road into a lay-by. How astonished the neighbours would have been if they could have seen us, so soon after this great send-off, sitting in the caravan in a roadside lay-by only a couple of miles down the road, eating our lunch. I had in mind a few quick sandwiches, but the girls wanted beans on toast, which they 'helped' me cook on our new-fangled gaz cooker and grill.

Once we were on the move again, and only then, did I relax and let myself believe that it was all really happening. We had burned our boats, the keys of our house had been handed over to the Canadian Professor, and here we were, driving south, pulling our caravan home behind us.

With the shedding of the walls of a house, life suddenly took on an entirely new dimension. It was a slightly scary feeling, but liberating, and I breathed in deeply this new heady oxygen of freedom. So many possibilities presented themselves, which had simply not existed before. We all felt it. The girls, buzzing with excitement, kept looking out of the back window just to make sure the caravan was still really there. Richard, at the wheel, was singing his own peculiar version of 'La Vie en Rose'. I joined in enthusiastically. He and I wished one another 'Bonne Route!', 'Bon Voyage!' 'Roulez-vous bien' and 'A la France', indeed all the French expressions that we could think of to say 'Have a wonderful journey'.

Our wonderful adventure had begun at last. We had given ourselves all of September to drive to Provence, to find a suitable place for the caravan in Aix and to settle in to our new life before Richard's University term began early in October. So we were in no great hurry to complete the journey. We could afford the time to savour the excitement of such a momentous experience.

The drive through England was exciting enough, if uneventful. We stopped again about six o'clock in a motor-way service station, where we had supper. I had prepared a cold roast chicken and salad for the meal in advance but first I heated a large tin of tomato soup on the gaz cooker, an activity which still had novelty value for the girls. They watched, fascinated, as plates appeared from the neat little cupboards above the cooker, and Katharine once again helped by counting out four knives, forks and spoons and setting them out on the little table.

Richard meanwhile had gone to buy a last English maga-zine or two and some chewy sweets and drinks for the journey next day and when he reappeared at the door the soup was all but served. The girls had already seated them-selves at the table and I was just about to sit down when Richard slipped into the remaining place, accidentally kicking the leg away from under the table as he did so and sending hot red soup sloshing over our knees. Fortunately, the soup was not boiling hot, but it created a lot of noise from the shrieking children, and a terrible mess – and nothing is more messy than tomato soup.

We emerged from the caravan, a noisy, gory foursome, somewhat to the astonishment of the surrounding motorists, and after removing the trickling soup with a towel from the children's legs and clothes, I checked that they were not scalded. Richard went inside and mopped up the table, seats and floor and disposed of what remained of the ill-fated first course of our meal.

Now fully recovered from the shock, the children were still outside, laughing at the spectacle they still presented. It looked like a family massacre, but no-one had actually suffered any harm. So we climbed back inside the caravan and a quick sponge down and change of clothes soon had us back at the table eating our chicken salad, none the worse for our adventure.

After that, Alison slept for most of the rest of the journey to Dover where we camped overnight. Katharine, who had somehow kept awake so far, determined to miss nothing of the journey, was happy to settle down in her enchantingly different double bed, even if she had to endure the indignity of sharing it with 'little sister'. We kissed her good night and watched as, feeling pretty in her new pyjamas, she walked around the bed, and pulled the curtains across each of the three windows of her new bedroom, but she took particular pleasure in drawing across the fourth long curtain which closed her off from the rest of the caravan, waving to us from her 'stage' before she disappeared.

It was like the end of a performance, and indeed it felt like the end of a chapter of our lives as we thought of leaving England with our little family tomorrow. But Richard and I were too exhausted by our journey to think too deeply about this and after putting together and making our bed we slept soundly at the other end of the caravan that night, to be awakened only by the alarm clock at eight o'clock next morning.

We took more care with the table leg that breakfast time and ever after it was a family joke to sing 'There'll be tomato soup all over the white cliffs of Dover...'

The showers at the Dover campsite were well used that morning and we were a very clean family as we drove on to the ferry for our journey across the channel.

From the deck we watched the white cliffs of England fade in the distance and we felt the excitement mount. This was no ordinary family going on holiday for a few weeks to France. We were migrating for a year. Who knew what might happen in that time.

The girls enjoyed the experience of sailing across to the Continent and made good use of all the facilities on board, insisting on visiting every corner of every deck. They spent their pocket money in the shop on sweets and drinks for the journey. I thought of the months ahead, and bought them a few more books.

Once we had the channel crossing behind us, and we were at last in France, we set off merrily on our way south.

Richard was used to driving on the right and as far as he was concerned there was just one more obstacle to be overcome before we could relax and enjoy the journey.

This obstacle was the Périphérique, the multi-lane ring road around Paris, which would have been a frightening prospect for us at any time, but with a caravan behind the car it was terrifying. With Richard driving, I was appointed navigator, and when at last I saw the sign for the Route National southwards, I shouted to Richard, who somehow moved across the speeding lines of traffic into the filter lane and we gratefully made our exit.

Having successfully negotiated this traffic nightmare, however, we decided to avoid the busy Autoroutes where possible, in favour of quieter and more interesting roads through the towns and villages of France, which Richard had plotted on our map.

It didn't matter too much that we would take a few days longer on the journey. There was, after all, no hurry. We enjoyed the feeling of migrating South from Britain, like the swallows, to winter in a warmer climate, and as each day took us closer to our destination, the sun shone more intensely and the terrain and the vegetation became more exotic.

Acres of ripening maize, taller than any adult, lined the country roads as we drove along. Field after field of giant sunflowers, their faces all turned to the sun, delighted the girls who had only ever seen these exotic flowers in ones and twos before. Vegetables of all descriptions, including artichokes, haricot verts, aubergines and courgettes grew in fields alongside the roads in profusion and plenty, promising delicious meals in the months ahead, when we would have the time to do them justice, both in cooking and eating.

Farther south, roadside vendors displaying trays of peaches and plums, apricots and nectarines, tempted us to stop and buy their exotic fruit. Melons too. We had never seen melons growing in the fields before, and that was something we all found fascinating. Even the humble tomato, which in England we had only ever seen grow in greenhouses, grew here on spindly stalks in the open fields.

We watched farmers harvesting the vines, which covered fields and hillsides, heavily laden with ripe bunches of grapes. Along country roads we followed the loaded trailers of grapes behind their tractors to the Co-operatives, where we once were allowed inside briefly to watch the great wine-presses crush the grapes in the first step of the process of wine making. Now we really felt we were in the warm south, and not for the first time on this journey, we were reminded of lines from Keats' poem, *Ode to Autumn*. 'Oh for a beaker full of the warm south, with beaded bubbles winking at the brim'.

On the night before we reached the end of our journey I can remember driving in to a campsite and parking the caravan under the branches of a eucalyptus tree, which we could hear all night long, soughing above the caravan in the warm breeze. The air was heady with the scent of thyme and rosemary and we celebrated with a special bottle of sparkling white wine which all of us, including the girls, sipped giggling with 'Provencal mirth'.

It was a magical evening and we felt intoxicated with the romance of just over a week of gypsy life behind us and the prospect of all those wonderful months of freedom stretching ahead.

For me, never an enthusiastic housewife at the best of times, the release from the prison of four walls, housework and gardening was the stuff of dreams. Katharine, aged four, had not yet started school, and Alison was only two, so this was the ideal opportunity for us all as a family to escape, before the prison bars of school began to close around the girls. Meantime, the two of them had adapted to gypsy life as easily as Richard and I had done, regarding it all as a great adventure.

CHAPTER THREE

AIX-EN-PROVENCE

High on excitement, we arrived on the outskirts of Aix the next afternoon, and though I dearly wanted to see the lovely town that I glimpsed from the Rotonde, a busy roundabout that encircled an imposing fountain, I realised that this was not the moment. I had to content myself with the thought that we would have plenty of time to explore the town once we had found a place for the caravan. Richard had obviously had enough of driving with a caravan behind us. It had been a great responsibility and now that we had arrived in Aix, our first priority was to find a suitable campsite which was to be our home for the long months ahead.

We followed the road signs which led us to Camping Les Arcs, at the foot of a hill on the edge of the town. From what we could see at the entrance it looked promising, with a large swimming pool and plenty of shady trees.

'This will do, won't it?' said Richard, and, only too glad to think of settling down at last in one place, I readily agreed.

We booked in and were directed to an emplacement near the banks of a river. At this time of year there were still some holidaymakers about but the summer crowds of campers had disappeared with the end of the school holidays and there was plenty of space to spread ourselves around. But that was for later. Right now, hot and dusty from our journey, all we wanted was a long cool swim. We had a quick shower, and then – splash. Richard dived in and came up grinning, his hair plastered to his head.

'It's fabulous,' he called, and we didn't need a second invitation. All four of us were soon splashing about and enjoying the cool water and the thought that at last we had arrived. Soon we were drying off on the patio, enjoying the afternoon sun, and I was beginning to plan ahead.

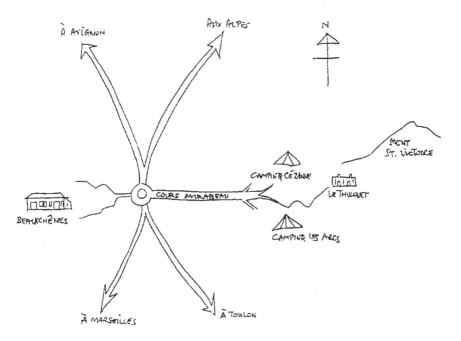

'I'm going to take you all into town for a meal', said Richard. 'I know you are dying to see what it's like and so am I. We can go shopping for food and all that sort of thing tomorrow.

'Great idea. Just what I was going to suggest,' I replied. 'What do you think, kids?'

'Yeeeessss!' came the enthusiastic shout from both girls.

There were not many people around the pool but Richard, keen as always to use his French, struck up a conversation with a French couple who were sunbathing nearby. They were very impressed with his command of their language and interested to hear that we were all planning to live in the caravan during the year while he was studying at the University in Aix. They introduced themselves as Monsieur and Madame Becker and told us that they lived on the delta of the River Rhone, where Monsieur Becker was employed as the Chief Engineer.

They talked to us about what we should see in and around Aix, which they said was one of their favourite places. When we asked them to recommend a good restaurant they told us to go to the Cours Mirabeau, right in the centre of town, which in their opinion was one of the most beautiful streets in Europe, and there we could find many excellent Restaurants and Cafes. Later, when Madame Becker saw that we were packing up our bathing towels she spoke quietly to her husband and then turned to us.

'It has been so nice to meet you,' she said. Unfortunately we are going home tomorrow, but we would like to invite you to our home. Would you like to come for lunch on Sunday? It would be interesting for you to see where we live, and this is our way to welcome you to our country.'

We thanked her for this charming invitation, which of course we were delighted to accept. What hospitable people the French were turning out to be, and we had only just arrived.

Later that evening, we dressed up and drove into town. We found a place to park the car and walked through narrow streets and quiet squares until we turned a corner into the Cours Mirabeau. 'Wow!' I gasped. The scene before us was breathtakingly beautiful. A wide boulevard, almost a square with pavements overhung by shady plane trees lining each side of a central thoroughfare. At the far end I could see through the trees the fountain of the Rotonde, which we had passed earlier in the day, and there were three smaller fountains at intervals along the central avenue.

As we walked along the wide shady pavement on one side of the Cours, we passed elegant houses, with massive carved figures flanking their imposing doorways. These were now smart hotels, banks and Insurance Offices, but we later read that in the eighteenth century they had been built as the homes of the rich businessmen of Aix.

Crossing to the other, rather busier side of the street, we joined the crowds shopping in the colourful boutiques and bookshops. I wanted to look in the shop windows, but the rest of the family were getting hungry and were making a beeline for the Restaurants and pavement Cafes that the Beckers had told us about. We found a table under a gaily striped parasol and, fascinated by the scene that surrounded us, we ordered our meal and sat back to enjoy our first drink while we watched the world go by.

It was a good time to be in the Cours Mirabeau as this was the hour of the promenade. Elegant French women, young and old, walked past, fashionably dressed in long skirts and dresses that were then a la mode. The men too were smartly dressed and looked very dignified. It was easy to distinguish between the fashion-conscious French and the foreign students who were dressed in the usual student garb of jeans and casual clothing. It was a warm evening and we basked in the dappled light beneath the trees, enjoying the first of many meals we were to eat in that wonderful setting over the following months.

Later, on our way back to the car we had a closer look at the lovely fountains that line the Cours. The girls especially liked the Rotonde, the fountain's splendid plumes of water sparkling and splashing in the late evening sunlight, but the older, less showy fountains were in many ways more interesting. At one ancient stone fountain several people were filling their empty bottles with the trickle of water that flowed from the fountain. They told us that the fountain dated from Roman times and that the water had health-giving properties, which had made Aix a spa town and been the basis of its prosperity centuries before.

In the following days we explored further and found many lovely squares and interesting buildings, museums and art galleries, including the home of the artist Paul Cézanne, probably the most famous son of Aix, who was one of the first of the cubist school of painters.

Meantime, we were settling in to life in the campsite, and getting to know one or two people. In particular, we made the acquaintance of an Englishman called Nigel who had a caravan nearby. He introduced himself soon after we arrived and told us that he had been living in his caravan ever since he had had a 'spot of bother' en route to Australia about five years previously. The 'spot of bother', we were later to discover, was his typical English under-statement for a major tragedy. Soon after reaching this very campsite, his wife had suddenly taken ill with a heart attack and been rushed to the local hospital in Aix, but she was pronounced dead on arrival at the hospital. Monsieur and Madame Delors, the owners of the site had been so kind and understanding to him in his distress at his sud-den bereavement that he had abandoned all idea of carry-ing on to Australia or anywhere else, and had simply stayed where he was. By now, five years later, he was a firmly established resident in Camping Les Arcs.

His caravan had become his permanent home, which he had made very comfortable. 'An Englishman's home is his castle' he declared rather predictably, 'and this is mine now'. He seemed content with his lot and had no desire to return to England or to move on elsewhere. He was, he told us, a self-employed cartographer and when he heard of our journey, which apart from the Paris Périphérique, we had enjoyed, he showed us some of the routes he had designed for people wishing to travel through France without touching Paris or other big cities.

He explained to us that the bridge with three arches, after which the campsite was named, was the subject of a famous painting by Winston Churchill, a fact which attracted numerous British tourists to visit the Campsite every year.

Nigel was obviously a lonely man, and after the girls had gone to sleep each evening in their curtained bed, he would come over to join us in our caravan where, over a bottle or two of wine he would tell us the next episode of the fascinating story of his life. We soon discovered that during the course of his life there had been many 'spots of bother'.

He had been cheated, disappointed and generally disil-lusioned by an alarming number of his fellow men. We began to understand why, when his wife had died in

France and he had experienced real sympathy and kindness from the campsite owners, Monsieur and Madame Delors, who were, after all, relative strangers, he had decided to put down roots here in this campsite in order to remain close to the warm hearted people who ran it.

Although he obviously enjoyed living in France, he had not found it easy to get to know many of the local people. 'They're all right, but you'll never get an invitation into any of their houses, you know,' he warned darkly. How surprised he was to hear that we had already been invited to lunch the following Sunday at the home of the Beckers, a couple whom we had met casually at the swimming pool the day after we arrived. They were now back home, repeating their invitation before they said 'Au Revoir.'

ARRIVÉE A AIX

CHAPTER FOUR

FRENCH HOSPITALITY

So it was that early the following Sunday morning we set out for St. Marie de la Mer, the town near where they lived on the delta of the Rhone. Monsieur Becker had told us that he was Chief Engineer on the Rhone Delta.

It was a very humid, sultry day and as we drove south-wards towards the delta, clouds began to form, and a brisk wind blew up, the famous Mistral. By the time we reached the coast this wind had whipped the dry sand from this vast area of beach and delta into a virtual sandstorm, reminding us vividly of the 'ghiblis' of Northern Africa, which blew sand from the Sahara Desert.

We arrived at the Becker's rather grand villa to find that the shutters had all been closed against the Mistral, 'to keep out the sand', as Madame Becker explained.

Unfortunately, this also excluded any breath of air, and despite the use of ceiling fans, the atmosphere within the house was almost suffocating. But so far we were all still surviving the heat and the sand, the girls actually finding it all very exciting, and greedy little souls that they were, looking forward to a delicious French meal. And they got it!

First of all, of course, came the aperitifs, Dubonnet on ice for Richard and me, orange juice for Katharine and Alison, who also tucked in to nuts and nibbles, for they this time they were ravenous. Soon we were seated at the splendid table in the dining room, its fine china and shin-ing silver flanked by numerous crystal wine-glasses, glit-tering in the candlelight from the branched silver candle-sticks in the gloom of the shuttered room.

Madame Becker entered with a huge circular plate of hors d'oeuvres, rainbow coloured with fresh green lettuce curling between red and yellow peppers, tiny tomatoes, creamy mayonnaise covered eggs and rolls of parma ham through which peeped the tips of fresh green asparagus.

It all looked marvellously inviting, and when Madame urged us to help ourselves, we didn't need a second bidding. Oh how good those first mouthfuls tasted. 'Another helping?' Well, why not?

The second course followed. Moules Marinieres, which we all loved, but Madam Becker's Moules Marinieres was even more delicious than usual, and soon the empty blue shells were heaping up on our plates, so that the flushed little faces of the girls could hardly been seen over them.

An excellent white wine accompanied the Moules, and we were just sitting back after this course when the entrée arrived. Everything we had eaten so far paled into insignificance at the first melting mouthful of Madame's 'Filet Mignon', and the aubergine sauce which accompanied it was the most sublime that I had ever tasted. There were vegetables of course, tiny potatoes, carrots, crunchy broccoli, all favourites of mine, but sadly, I could eat no more. I tried some of the superb red wine, which was served with this course, hoping to find a space for the rest of the meal, but halfway through the Filet Mignon I found I simply couldn't eat another mouthful. The girls had given up long before me, and we watched enviously as Richard and our hosts enjoyed the dessert, a glazed strawberry flan with lashings of cream, and yet another wine.

This was followed by the cheese board on which were arranged marvellous French cheeses, Roquefort, Brie, Camembert, and others. Even Richard was beaten by now, and remembering that he would soon have to drive us home, he turned down the offer of brandy in favour of a sobering cup of coffee.

It was well past four o'clock when, replete, we staggered from the dining room to the lounge, where coffee was served. It was long past the hour when Alison usually had her siesta. Hot, sleepy and overfed, she climbed on my knee and curled up, closing her eyes and sucking her thumb.

'Ah pauvre!' cooed Monsieur Becker, coming close to

kiss her. At this, Alison, overwhelmed by too much food and the strangeness of everything, howled her objection, tears rolling down her blazing face.

'Never mind,' soothed Madame Becker. 'She will enjoy the drive.'

'A surprise for you!' Monsieur Becker beamed. 'We are going to show you our beautiful countryside'.

I shot a look of alarm at Richard. We both knew all too well what was in store for us and our kind, well-meaning hosts, but what could we do but acquiesce to their plan? It would be ungracious to refuse.

Outside it was a different world. The Mistral had died down and taken with it the sand and cloud, leaving a brilliantly clear atmosphere with dazzling sunlight and brilliant colours. Monsieur Becker laughed when we exclaimed at the transformation of the landscape.

'Ah oui, le Mistral is called 'le balailleur' the broom, because it sweeps everything clean and fresh.'

We set out in Monsieur Becker's car, crossed the Rhone Estuary in a car ferry, and then followed a lengthy tour of Arles and Nimes, and the surrounding countryside, which at any other time we would have thoroughly enjoyed.

At first all went well. The motion of the car sent Alison to sleep in my arms and I hoped this might last the journey. But it was too good to last. Katharine was squashed in the back seat between her father and me, and she too was hot and tired. She had fidgeted around and inevitably Alison woke up, squirmed about in my arms like a boa constrictor and put up a continuous howl of fury and fatigue which rendered all conversation hopeless, though Monsieur Becker did his best to point out the historic buildings and bridges which we saw on our long drive.

I remember we all got out at the Bull Ring in Arles and Mr. Becker surprised us by saying how much the French enjoyed bullfighting. We had imagined it was only the Spanish who enjoyed this bloodthirsty sport.

I heard little of the fascinating history of the area which Monsieur Becker tried to outline against the mounting war cry from the back seat, and it was with a feeling of relief that I realised we were at last on the return journey towards the river and eventually arrived at the Becker's home. It had been a long afternoon.

We took our leave of the Beckers shortly afterwards, thanking them for their splendid hospitality. It was only when Alison got back in her familiar seat in our car that she stopped grizzling like an angry bear cub and finally fell asleep. Katharine too, hot and exhausted, was soon sleeping peacefully and the journey home was blessedly quiet.

Next day when we told our neighbour Nigel about the day of dramatic contrasts in the weather, in the scenery and the very special meal, he was surprised. Realising that he was also very envious, we played down the significance of our experience, although we had really been overwhelmed by it.

We told him that he was an inspiration to us, that we admired the way he had made a life for himself here and that he had encouraged us to feel we should be able to survive a year in this place.

CHAPTER FIVE

CAMPING CÉZANNE

However, it was not to be. A few days later, Richard came back from a reconnaissance around Aix and announced that we were moving.

'Oh, No!' said Katharine, who had already made friends on the campsite, and I felt something of her dismay. But Richard was adamant and I agreed at least to go and see the new location, which he was enthusing about – 'Camping Cézanne'.

It wasn't far away. We drove up a long hill from our present situation by the river through Val St. André and a few hundred metres beyond to where 'Camping Cézanne' announced itself. We looked eagerly through the windows as Richard drove us through the gates, past the office and Restaurant, then on, on uphill, past tents and caravans on several levels, well shaded by tall cherry trees.

We passed a large rambling house, and several more levels of tents and caravans, on up to the top of the hill, where we found a large pond and a swimming pool at the end of an avenue of tall poplar trees. The car stopped and we tumbled out and looked around.

'Well?' Richard asked impatiently, his arms sweeping around the panorama which at this height was suddenly revealed. 'What do you think of it?

A glorious landscape stretched in front of us, high above the town, with lines of poplar trees immediately below, obscuring the view of caravans and tents but revealing a sweep of countryside to the south. Beyond some fields and rolling hills to the east, the red roofs of a small village peeped through clumps of trees. Above the village rose the splendid summit of Mont St. Victoire, familiar to us as the subject of many wonderful paintings by Cézanne. Hence the name of the campsite.

Now I could understand why Richard had insisted on bringing us up here. The feeling of space and light was overpowering and suddenly I realised how gloomy and confined we were in our position by the river in Camping Les Arcs.

'Oh yes, it's brilliant up here. I love it. When can we move?'

Relieved that I agreed with him, Richard informed me that, hoping I would agree to the move, he had already spoken to Monsieur Dubois, the proprietor of the campsite,

CAMPING CÉZANNE

which was in fact still a thriving cherry farm. Monsieur Dubois was also the owner of the large house, which we had seen on our way up the hill, and in which he lived with his wife, his daughter and seven sons. An agreement had been reached between them about what we should pay for a stay of several months, and Richard proudly showed us the place he had chosen for our caravan under a line of poplar trees, where we could look out from our windows at an uninterrupted view of Mont St. Victoire. Nearby was a play area for the girls. Katharine was already trying out the swings, while Alison was happily scuffing about in the sandpit.

After that there was no contest. As we had all been won over so completely there seemed no reason to delay the move, and the very next day we said 'Au Revoir' to the proprietors of Camping Les Arcs, and assuring our friend Nigel that he was welcome to come and see us in our new location, we hitched up our caravan and moved up the hill to the sunny heights of Camping Cézanne.

The girls quickly settled down, and with the fickleness of childhood, they cheerfully made new friends, the grandchildren of Monsieur Dubois, with whom they quickly learned to communicate in French, and both Katharine and Alison could be heard calling 'Valerrrrrie', rolling their r's in true French fashion.

On the first day they found a water tap coming out of the mouth of a grinning lion's mouth which Katharine immediately called 'The Happy Lion', after one of her favourite bedtime stories. Listening to this story, and as many other favourites as they could persuade Richard or me to read to them each evening, the two girls would fall asleep in their cosy double bed, curtained off from the rest of the caravan, and usually it was only the noise of breakfast being made that woke them up.

After breakfast, they tumbled out of the caravan to play with their new friends till lunchtime. Then, after a brief siesta they were out again. By the time Richard's University term began they looked like gypsy children. Katharine, our little redhead, was covered in freckles and Alison's blonde hair had bleached white in the sun. The Dubois family exclaimed at their unusual colouring. 'Comme elles sont mignons! ' they said, calling Katharine 'La Rousse' and Alison 'Blondinette'.

Once the University term began, our lives took on a more regular pattern. Monsieur Dubois and his wife urged us to send Katharine to Maternelle in Val St. André. They were justly proud of the excellent pre-school facilities that the French system provided and which their own grandchildren enjoyed.

We took their advice, and when we went to the Maternelle we were warmly welcomed. Katharine had already been to Nursery school in England, but here, because no one spoke her language, the teacher, Madame Mesurier, suggested that I should come to the school with Katharine during the first week to help her settle in.

Alison came along too, of course, and for a week we all joined in the activity of this excellent school, which I found extremely interesting, not least because by helping with the French children, I was learning the language. Madame Mesurier was a very experienced teacher and knew how to entertain and teach small children. On one occasion she showed them how to make Potage de légumes – vegetable soup. They watched and listened to her while she prepared the vegetables, they learned the vocabulary, which she wrote up on the blackboard, and of course at the end of the lesson they enjoyed the delicious soup. Katharine loved the school and quickly made friends, while Alison was delighted to be there with all the other children.

The week flew happily by and the following Monday morning, with all the other French mothers, I arrived with my children at the gates of the Maternelle – and then the trouble started. I had warned Alison that we would not be going in with Katharine this morning, and she seemed to understand and accept the situation. But when Madame Mesurier met us, she took Katharine by the hand and shut the gate with a dreadful clang.

Suddenly Alison realised she was shut out of all the fun, and she lifted her head and howled to get in and join her sister. Hearing her cries, Katharine turned around, and tearing herself away from Madame, ran back to the gate, crying to get out to Alison.

There was I, almost in tears myself, while my two little girls clutched at each other through the iron bars of the gate, one crying to get in, the other to get out.

As the French mothers and children looked on at 'les Anglaises' in astonishment, Madame whisked Katharine up in her arms, and with a wave and a reassuring smile over her shoulder at me, she disappeared into the building. I lifted the sobbing Alison into my arms and hugged her tightly, until eventually she calmed down sufficiently to walk home with me, both of us feeling rather forlorn.

Home, of course, was the caravan and waiting there for us were the usual chores, but with a difference. That morning, to take her mind off her sister's absence, I asked Alison to help with the housework, and she was soon busy with her favourite task of lining up her dolls and teddy bears on the pillows in her bed, and then with a little help from me, she made her bed. After washing up in my 'kitchen' I allowed her to help me dry the dishes, after which she trotted to and fro, clearing away all the food from the breakfast table. I swept out the caravan with a broom and tidied our 'bedroom', which had earlier been transformed into the table and benches.

As all memories of the morning's trauma seemed to have been forgotten, I found a colouring book and crayons and this kept Alison busily engaged at the table until it was time for 'elevenses', usually orange juice and biscuits. By this time Mr. Dubois' grandchildren were out playing by the swings and sandpit, and Alison happily joined them for the rest of the morning.

This was the pattern of most mornings, but sometimes we had to take the washing to the launderette down in Val St. André, and there too we bought our food at the delightful shops that can be found in any French village; the Boulangerie with its wonderful Baguettes and Flutes, Pain de Campagne and croissants; the Patisserie whose front window was like a still life painting with deliciously glazed 'tartes aux fraises' and irresistable 'gateaux' of every conceivable variety. But best of all was the open market in Val St. André, where we could buy fresh fruit and vegetables every day. I decided that now was the time for the family to become vegetarian and I tried everything from Jerusalem Artichokes to Asparagus, from pumpkin soup to ratatouille. I told the family it was our vegetarian voyage of discovery and for a time they were willing voyageurs. However, the novelty quickly wore off and soon they were begging for sausages, spaghetti bolognese, stew, rosbif, anything with meat in it. I caved in, not least because I was running out of inspiration and marched along to the Boucherie where I quickly found that the meat, though more expensive than in England, was of excellent quality and totally free of fat. The French butchers have the pride and precision of surgeons in presenting their wares.

The Supermarkets were too far away for Alison and me to walk to, never mind carry heavy bags of shopping back home, so we had a family trip to Monoprix or Super-marché Leclerc once or twice a week when Richard didn't need the car.

On one such occasion I was looking for something on the shelves and for a moment absent-mindedly I left Katharine with the trolley, inside which Alison was sitting. At first there was a great deal of giggling which suddenly stopped, followed by an ominous silence. I hurried back to where I had left the girls, to find Alison sitting in the trol-ley, looking guilty, while Katharine and a few amused bystanders stood looking at a little pool of liquid on the floor under the trolley. I could guess what had happened, but Katharine, when I pressed her, reluctantly admitted that she had been 'twirling' the trolley round and round, making Alison laugh so much that she wet herself – which explained the pool of liquid. Mortified, I apologised to the assistant and offered to mop it up. 'Ca ne fait rien,' she replied, fetched a bucket of water and mopped up the puddle without complaint, but I had learned my lesson. That was the last time I left my children alone with a supermarket trolley, even for a moment.

On another occasion in a bookshop my girls disgraced themselves by giggling uncontrollably about something silly, and when I told them to be quiet and apologised to the French salesman, he said how delightful it was to hear children enjoying themselves so much.

The French children would never have behaved in such an unseemly manner. We were often impressed with the maturity of even quite small French children. During that year in France, having left our girls with a baby sitter,

Richard and I often went to dinner parties with French families late in the evening, to see children as young as Katharine sit quietly throughout the meal, dressed in pretty frocks, solemnly listening to the adult conversation, and even drinking a glass of wine and water with their meal.

We were invited, all four of us, to dinner one evening with the Dubois family. Monsieur Dubois had asked Richard to give his youngest son, Henri, English lessons and he wanted to get to know us better. The big Dubois family was seated with us around the dining table, Madame had produced a marvellous meal and we were enjoying the wine and the conversation when Monsieur Dubois asked Richard what part of England we came from. When Richard answered 'Yorkshire', his host became very animated.

'Yorkshire', he exclaimed. 'But – le Yorkshire is the best pig in the world.'

He thought to himself for a moment, obviously excited. 'Richard, I would be very grateful if you would bring me one of these Yorkshire pigs. I have wanted this pig for my farm for many years. Please can you do this for me.'

Richard was obviously not too sure how he might achieve this, but nevertheless he agreed to look into the possibility and with this Monsieur Dubois appeared to be content.

While I understood much of what was being said during the meal, I did not dare participate beyond a very basic level, because of my lack of confidence in speaking the language. As the weeks went by we got to know more and more French people and were invited to their homes and the same pattern repeated itself. Richard carried on conversations in fluent French throughout the evenings and I said as little as possible. By November, I was thoroughly sick of sitting quietly and I realised it was time to do something about improving my French. I decided to attend classes on two afternoons a week at the Institut pour Etudiants Etrangers, (Institute for Foreign Students) in Aix.

On Tuesday we studied French Grammar in the old fashioned way, declensions, conjugations, endless verb tenses and vocabulary, but it didn't help my oral French at all as we students rarely uttered a word. The Professeur intoned from his dais and chalked on the blackboard, while we scribbled in our exercise books like good children – though the youngest there were American Students aged about twenty from North Carolina. And we were given homework. Heaps of it! Translations, lists of vocabulary to learn and essays to write.

The Thursday lesson was French Literature, and here again we sat mute while the voice of Monsieur le Professeur droned through the long afternoons on works by Stendhal, Gide, Maupassant, Moliere. I loved the literature but more than once, chin propped on hand, I drifted off to sleep, to be rudely awoken when my hand slipped, and my head nearly thumped on to the desk.

However, at least I was listening to spoken French and refreshing my dormant knowledge of vocabulary, grammar and literature. Besides, it was good for me to get out there and meet people, while Richard stayed with the children on his two free afternoons. He loved this chance of being with his daughters and he and the girls had fun together.

On one occasion, however, I returned from my afternoon Literature class to find to my horror that Richard had decided to cut Alison's hair. I took one look at the urchin who, only a few hours ago had been my adorable little toddler with pretty blond tendrils of hair framing her sweet face and I cried with anger.

'What have you done? It's horrible!' I could not find adequate words to express my sense of loss as I lifted the shorn Alison and stroked what hair remained on her head.

Richard looked crestfallen. 'It was such a sticky afternoon. Alison was too hot. I thought it would be cooler, more comfortable for her...' he trailed off, lamely.

'Daddy put a bowl on her head,' Katharine volunteered, obviously fascinated by the whole operation.

'Oh, my God,' I howled. 'A bowl! Well, it looks like it. How could you do such a thing? What on earth possessed you? Why didn't you wait till I got home?'

'Oh, it's not the end of the world, for goodness sake,' protested Richard. 'Her hair will grow again.' At this point I nearly threw something at him but there was nothing suitable to hand.

I was so mad with Richard that I could hardly speak to him for the rest of the day, but by next morning my anger had cooled. There was nothing I could do about it now anyway. It was a fait accompli. I could only thank heaven that he hadn't cut Katharine's lovely red hair. I found out afterwards from him that he thought about it, but took fright when he saw the results of his handiwork on poor little Alison.

At the Institut I met Janet, a young English woman who was overjoyed to find a compatriot and promptly invited us to her home to meet her family. She was married to Jean-Marc, a French Engineer, whose job as Clerk of Works on various building projects took him away from home for long periods. They had two children, a three year old boy named Jacques and a five year old girl Pascale, who became firm friends with my girls. They lived in a large airy ground floor apartment surrounded by well kept gardens on the edge of the town.

Janet came to see me one afternoon at the caravan and was astonished to find me sitting at the table with Alison, reading her a story. 'Why don't you send Alison to Garderie? ' she asked.

I knew that during term time her little boy, Jacques, was at Garderie and the girl Pascale was at Maternelle. In the school holidays they went to summer camp. She couldn't understand that I didn't want to send my children away, that I really enjoyed their company in the few precious years they would be with me before they went to school.

Janet told me that she suffered from Agoraphobia, a fear of leaving the house on her own, and she said she even found shopping in the local supermarket difficult. She wasn't very happy living in France. Jean-Marc was away so much, and she found it difficult to make friends with the French women she knew. 'I've been here for years and they still call me 'Madame', she wailed.

'All the more reason for keeping your children at home!' I argued, but she wouldn't hear of it. When in France, one did as the French did, and all of the mothers sent their children to the Garderie as soon as possible and when they reached the age of four they went to the Maternelle. Even in the holidays many children, including Janet's little boy and girl, went away from home to summer camps. It was an excellent system, which has been the envy of many other countries, but I felt that in Janet's case, she might have felt less lonely if she had had less childminding support and more daily contact with her own children.

In November Janet persuaded Jean-Marc to take her and the children back to England for two weeks' holiday, and when she asked us to look after the apartment and the dog, Bruno, during their absence, we readily agreed.

This was a pleasant break for us from life on the campsite and the apartment seemed enormous to us, and very luxurious. We particularly enjoyed soaking in the bathtub, a luxury we didn't have on the campsite, where we could only have showers. The children played with all the gorgeous toys that Pascale and Richard had in their rooms and they enjoyed watching children's television, which they hadn't seen since leaving home.

We were less willing to return to the habit of sitting in front of the box, but I remember watching one programme where the presenter was comparing the French and the English sense of humour. In one sequence he pedantically explained why the English found the comedians Morecambe and Wise so funny. As the sequence showed the two comically trying to climb into the same leg of a pair of trousers, with predictably ludicrous results, we felt sure that the French audience would have no difficulty in seeing the humour in this hilarious situation.

Just for fun, Richard and I were in the habit of making literal translations of colloquial English expressions into French. For example, when it was raining hard one of us might say 'Il pleut chats et chiens' – 'It's raining cats and dogs'. This would reduce us to helpless laughter. How surprised we were one evening when watching a French film to hear the hero say to another character 'Je suis malade comme un perroquet.' – 'I'm as sick as a parrot.' Maybe we shared more colloquialisms with the French than we realised.

We really enjoyed taking Bruno, Janet's Dalmation, for long walks and the girls loved his habit of leaping from the garden through the open windows of the flat, landing with a great thump in the middle of the lounge. We all became very fond of Bruno, and missed him more than anything else when we left the apartment and returned to our caravan when Janet and Jean Marc came back from holiday.

At the campsite the Dubois boys also had a Dalmation called Saturn. We often saw this beautiful dog streaking across the wide-open spaces of the camp with one or more of the Dubois brothers chasing behind. On one occasion we realised that the dog was chasing a rabbit and later to our horror we realised that this poor creature was one of the dozen or so rabbits that the family raised in cages for eating. The cages were in the middle of the campsite and our children loved to go sometimes to see the rabbits, which they thought were pets, like the white rabbit they once had back at home.

When Richard realised that the boys were releasing the rabbits and setting the dog on them, he took them aside and pointed out the cruelty of such an uneven chase. They were fond of Richard, who sometimes played football with them in the evenings, and promised not to let Saturn chase the rabbits again. However, we never told the girls that the sweet little rabbits were destined for the dinner table.

One morning the Dubois boys were very excited. The news that day was the death of President de Gaulle. I remember them running around shouting 'De Gaulle est mort. Vive de Gaulle.' In common with many students at that time, the boys were very left wing and they shed no tears for the right-wing President.

On another occasion the boys told us that their house had been burgled. The police had been called and the main suspects were some Moroccan immigrants who had been seen in the vicinity. France was even then beginning to have problems with immigration from their former colonies Morocco and Algeria.

We had some American friends who told us that they had gone out for the evening, leaving a French girl student to baby- sit in their house in the countryside near Aix. When they returned later that evening the house was locked and barred and they had to knock for some time before the student opened the door to let them in. They laughed and asked her why she had barricaded herself in the house in this manner. They themselves left doors and windows open all the time in a country that they considered a hundred times safer than the U.S.A.

She looked at them, aghast, and said 'Are you mad. Don't you know that there are thieves and criminals everywhere and you are asking for trouble. Why do you think everyone has a big dog and high gates around their houses.'

This made me feel a little bit insecure in our caravan, but on the other hand, we thought, we were probably safer there than in an opulent house. However, even we were once shouted at by the left wing students as we passed them in our car and caravan, clearly marked GB. 'Capitalistes!', they shouted, obviously mistaking us for tourists, little knowing that we were students too, probably a lot poorer than themselves.

My friend Janet couldn't believe that anyone could exist in a caravan as we did for months on end. She obviously felt sorry for us, but in fact we loved the freedom of life in the open air in that beautiful place. The morning sunlight filtered through our flame-coloured curtains to wake us up to one lovely day after another. The girls went to bed in the warm light of sunset after glorious sunset. Whilst the late summer warmth continued we lived outdoors most of the time. We bathed in the swimming pool at the top of the hill. We ate our meals at a table under the trees. We read books in the sun while the children played nearby.

Alison often had her siesta in a hammock slung between nearby trees while I kept an eye on her from the windows of the caravan. More than once I saw a passing couple stop and look down wonderingly at the rosy-cheeked Alison, sleeping peacefully like a cherub in a medieval painting. It was truly a paradise and it seemed as if the summer would never end.

CHAPTER SIX

WINTER SETS IN

And then the weather broke. The blue skies disappeared for days on end behind angry clouds. The temperature plummeted. It rained – and rained. The dry caked earth of the campsite turned to sticky white mud, which was trampled into the caravan on to the floor and every other surface, which made it difficult to keep the caravan clean. By the end of November, when the weather turned really cold, with frosty nights, we realised how inadequately insulated the caravan was and we were faced with the prospect that we would have to abandon our gypsy life and seek warmer accommodation for the winter.

Fortunately, Monsieur Dubois had a solution. On the campsite were three small cottages, normally used for holiday rentals, and one of these was free. We moved in. It wasn't luxury but it was the best we could afford and at least it was better than freezing every night. There was only one bedroom, where we squeezed into two double beds, and a separate living room with a 'mazout'. This was the oil stove, which became the focal point of the house each evening, attracting less fortunate friends, usually students, who were seeking heat as well as company.

Two of these students, Dominique and Maurice, had asked to rent our caravan as soon as we moved out of it. They were a couple, devoted to one another and to extreme left-wing politics. They had been deeply involved in the student unrest that had convulsed the whole of France throughout 1968 and which continued to plague the Universities of France more than one year on. Sitting around the 'mazout' evening after evening that December, we had many lively debates with them on French and English politics.

One such evening we were thus engaged when a sinister individual turned up, hot foot from Paris, looking for Dominique and Maurice. He was a Communist agitator and organiser, who proceeded in rapid French to instruct our two friends on how to organise a demonstration in Aix University the following weekend.

We listened in disbelief, understanding enough of what was said to realise the import of what was going on in front of us. Eventually, when the urgent business of the visit had been dealt with, he turned to us and the discussion became more general.

He asked us about the political situation in England and more pointedly he asked us 'Why in Britain, a nation in which the Industrial Revolution began, a country which inspired Karl Marks and Engels, is there no viable Communist Party?'

Good question! After some heated discussion of British politics, we asked him why in France, the country of the French Revolution, now so full of protest and rebellion – why was there a right wing Goverment in power? He had no real answer to our question, except to reveal that there was no unity in the Communist movement in France, just several warring parties of the left.

That weekend we saw our charming friend Maurice, a powerful young man over six feet tall, standing alongside the diminutive blonde figure of Dominique, shouting revolution to the crowds of students. Indeed they did succeed in closing the University several times during that year, with sit-ins and demonstrations of varying forms which advanced their aims not a whit, but which certainly succeeded in preventing the progress of lectures for days on end.

In spite of their rather extreme political views, we found Dominique and Maurice very amusing company. They were lovers, and they defiantly declared to us that they would never marry. Marriage was for the petit bourgeoisie. They explained how marriage supported materialism, capitalism and the oppression of the masses, through unnecessary possessions such as houses, washing machines, television sets, cars and caravans. By persisting in owning such items we were supporting the capitalists of Europe.

We pointed out that there was more than one way of looking at the whole question. In Britain, a Socialist Government had decided to encourage poorer families to invest in their own homes by introducing the Option Mortgage Scheme. This scheme, in effect a subsidy, which had allowed us, even on a Student's Grant, to get a Mortgage on a new house in York, seemed fairer to us than paying rent to the rip-off landlords who preyed on the poor and on students in University towns.

Besides, we argued, wasn't it a bit hypocritical for them to criticise us for our ownership of the caravan in which they were living at a nominal rent? But the logic of this argument seemed to pass them by.

As December wore on, the cold nights in the caravan eventually drove them to find an apartment in Aix, and we were more than a little surprised to receive an invitation to their wedding. This invitation was the most contradictory document one could imagine. In a long opening harangue it began by decrying the 'capitalist' institution of marriage. Nevertheless, it went on, they had decided that their love for one another was so strong that they had decided to formalise it by getting married and we were invited to attend their civic wedding ceremony in Dominique's home-town of Nantes.

We were really sorry that for several reasons we were unable to attend the wedding, but when the newly married couple returned to the University we received an invitation to their new home. Glad to keep up our friendship with these interesting young people, we went along to their new address, which proved to be a modern apartment in an up-market area of Aix. They showed us proudly around their flat, which, to our astonishment, was equipped with all the latest electrical gadgetry, including a washing machine, a fridge, and a television set, all of which had been provided by their middle-class families.

By Christmas we were beginning to realise that we could not continue living in the cottage. The walls streamed with condensation and we all had dreadful colds and hacking coughs. Christmas lunch was a jovial occasion, to which we invited our friends, Marie and Roger, two French students who worked in the campsite reception for Monsieur Dubois. They lived in much worse conditions than ours, sleeping in the room behind the Reception Office, their living space screened off from the public gaze by a couple of blankets hitched over a rope.

Roger was a student of the Ecole Normale Superior, one of the most prestigious educational institutions in France, and one day he would probably find a high powered and high paid job in Government. Meantime, he lived in penury, his rich Parisian family having cut him off financially because he had married Marie, a delicate Fine-arts student, against the wishes of his parents. We were surprised to find that students in France were given no student grant as we were in Britain. Moreover, they had to pay high fees to their University, whereas at that time students' fees were paid automatically by the British Government. Marie and Roger had to live on what they earned by running the reception at Camping Cézanne. It wasn't riches, and they lived like church mice, but they were cheerfully determined to be together, whatever sacrifices had to be endured.

But there was no talk of sacrifices that Christmas Day, when they joined us in our cottage for Christmas lunch. In my oven I roasted a large chicken with stuffing, crispy bacon and roast potatoes, while Marie made a delicious French sauce to accompany the sprouts, carrots and other vegetables. It certainly looked delicious, but I had to take their word for it because I had caught a heavy cold and by Christmas I had completely lost my sense of taste. How frustrating to look at my plateful of scrumptious food, to eat it, to feel it going down my throat and yet not be able to taste a thing! The Christmas 'pudding', which Marie had prepared for dessert met the same sad fate, but at least I could see that everybody else enjoyed their Christmas lunch.

As we had a few weeks' holiday after Christmas, we decided to take the caravan to the French Riviera. The Mediterranean coast was only 30 miles south of Aix, and we were naturally interested in seeing as much of it as possible during our stay. So we planned our route to stay in Campsites near the famous places such as Cannes and Monte Carlo. These were usually tourist traps, to be avoided in the summer months, but we found the roads and beaches almost deserted in the dog days between Christmas and New Year.

We chugged lazily along quiet roads, passing dazzling white houses set against blue Mediterranean bays and palm fringed rocky outcrops. We camped above Cannes at Grasse, where in summer fields of lavender echoed the deep blue of the sky and filled the air with heady fragrance. Even now, in the dead of winter, it was exotic, the colours intense. We walked along the Boulevardes in Cannes, pretending to be millionaires, as we gazed at the splendid Hotels and Restaurants, the haunts of the rich and famous, which fringe the seafront.

At Monte Carlo we waited at the palace, hoping for a glimpse of Prince Ranier and his beautiful Princess, the former film star, Grace Kelly. Luck was with us and, to our delight, flashing by for one brief moment in the gleaming Rolls Royce we saw the blonde hair and lovely smiling face of Princess Grace with Prince Ranier sitting beside her. The girls were enchanted. It was like all their fairy tales come true, and from that moment on their holiday took on a new dimension. They had seen a fairy tale princess with her handsome prince, driving into their palace. They were even prepared to overlook the Rolls Royce although, strictly speaking, the princess should have been in a carriage drawn by white horses. But it was a white Rolls Royce, after all, and my daughters were very tolerant about such minor details.

As we walked past the famous Casino, much to Katharine's embarrassment, Richard sang lustily 'The man who broke the bank at Monte Carlo'. Fortunately the Casino was closed and he was therefore not tempted to try his luck at the tables.

Katharine particularly liked the miniature orange trees, now laden with oranges, which grew in large tubs outside the doors of the Casino. It was all very exotic. During the day, warmed by blazing sunshine, we picnicked on beaches, which in the summer would be heaving with humanity, but now were utterly deserted. We could almost imagine it was indeed summer but once the sun went down the temperature plummeted until at night it was well below zero and we were frozen in our unheated caravan.

At New Year we found ourselves in a surreal landscape, where the earth, the trees and shrubs were charred and blackened – obviously by fire. The name of the place, Mandelieu, seemed familiar, but the campsite where we stayed was deserted, apart from ourselves and one other caravan belonging to a German family, who reminded us that forest fires had blazed all around this area the previous summer, burning to the ground vast areas of forest and many luxurious homes.

So that was why the name Mandelieu had a familiar ring to it! We recalled the images of the forest fires on our television screens the previous summer, and the tragic story of local inhabitants fleeing from the blazing inferno. They were caught on the motorway between the hills, which acted like a wind tunnel, drawing the fire faster than their speeding cars, and in this ghastly manner several families lost their lives. The German family told us that the fire had been started deliberately by some youths, who had set alight a stolen car in the forests above Mandelieu.

Having imparted this gruesome tale, the Germans disappeared into their caravan, no doubt well insulated from the freezing temperatures outside, and we could hear them singing in the New Year in an alcoholic haze, while we drank the health of 'Absent friends' and sang Auld Lang

Syne over a lonely bottle of whisky, while the girls slept soundly.

'Mimicking Tony Hancock's plaintive voice, Richard said 'We've got friends all over the world – just none in Mandelieu.'

Soon after we joined the sleeping girls in their bed, as we found it warmer to sleep all together, like peas in a pod, thus conserving what warmth our bodies generated. There was a deep frost outside that night and by morning our windows were frozen into wonderful fern patterns. We stayed where we were, loath to climb out of our sleeping bags to brave the big freeze until the sun began to warm everything up again.

Before we could get up and face the day we tried to raise the temperature in the caravan by turning on the gas jets of the cooker. Then I put the porridge on to cook, and boiled the kettle for tea. Only when the steaming porridge was served would the others climb out of bed, but they soon cheered up when they consumed the hot tea, bacon and eggs and lots of hot buttered toast. The children were soon warmly dressed, running about outside and squealing with delight with Richard as he helped them make slides on the frosty tarmac.

SNOW IN PROVENCE

When we returned to Aix and drove through the gates
of Camping Cezanne, we found everything covered
in snow, a rare phenomenon in France, as Monsieur
Dubois assured us. The snow cover was hardly a centime-
tre in depth. However, with a layer of ice beneath the
snow, the hilly incline of the campsite terrain presented
an immediate problem. Pulling the heavy caravan, our car
was skidding on the slippery surface, and as we could get
no grip to climb the hill we were stuck just inside the
camp entrance.

Monsieur Dubois scratched his head at first. Then he
had a bright idea. 'Tiens!' he exclaimed. 'Attendez-moi!' We
had no alternative. We waited until he returned riding tri-
umphantly on his miniature tracteur! By now a crowd of
stalwarts had assembled – students, of course, and they
howled with laughter as Monsieur Dubois hitched our caravan to this little vehicle, and pulled – with no more suc-
cess than our car had had in moving the caravan. It was
like watching a flea trying to pull an elephant. In the end
even Monsieur Dubois had to admit defeat. We thanked
him and with his permission and the help of the onlookers
we manhandled the caravan into a space near the entrance
and, getting back into the car we returned to our little
house. What joy to have the mazout blazing once again
that night and to feel warm again in our own beds.

Next morning we found Monsieur Dubois busily at
work with a blazing blow-torch – on the pathway! When
we asked him what he was doing he huffed and puffed for
a while before admitting that the pipes had all frozen during the night and none of the showers or toilets were
working. He was evidently trying to de-freeze the pipes
buried underground with a blow-lamp! This desperate

ploy didn't work, of course, and later that day the hapless Monsieur Dubois assembled as many portable oil heaters as he could find to warm up the toilet block. Unfortunately some of these oil heaters were so ancient that they emitted thick black smoke which blackened the white walls of the toilet block.

Next morning Monsieur Dubois was to be seen in the block, looking like Al Jolson or one of the black and white minstrels, gingerly picking his way across the ice rink cre-

LA SOLUTION 'MAZOUT'

TOILETTES

ated overnight when the flooded floors froze. It was not until several days later, when the thaw set in, that the chaotic efforts of our landlord to beat the freeze at last relented. While we felt sorry for him, faced as he was with the bill for the damage caused by the ice, we couldn't help finding it all so hilarious that Richard created a series of cartoons with captions in French depicting the various phases of the saga, such as 'Il faut patiner dans les toilettes' – You must skate in the toilets. These cartoons afforded great amusement to Marie and Roger and indeed to all the other students on the campsite, who encouraged Richard to produce more cartoons and suggested other aspects of Monsieur Dubois' endearing and eccentric character which could lend themselves to the art of caricature.

It was just as well that we had some fun, albeit at the expense of Monsieur Dubois, because for some time it had been clear to Richard and me that we could not continue as we were. The cottage was damp and unhealthy, the walls streaming with condensation, and we all had dreadful colds and hacking coughs. We worried that our two little girls, who normally enjoyed the best of health, might become really ill in these damp conditions. It looked ominously as though I might have to go home with the girls to my mother's house, as our own was let for the year.

But before we faced this decision there was one straw that we clung to. Caroline, one of the French students from the University, knew about our problems and told us that she had an uncle, a Monsieur Colombe, who was about to leave his house in the country near Aix, to visit New Zealand. He planned to be away for at least three months, returning just after Easter, and he was looking for a caretaker, someone who would live in his house and look after it in his absence.

The Autoroute de Nice was being built in that period, bypassing Aix, and cutting through the countryside nearby. The autoroute was due to carve its way through Monsieur Colombe's land, cutting off at least half of the long drive up to the house and necessitating the felling of several ancient oak trees along the drive that lay in its path. Monsieur Colombe had protested, of course, trying desperately to prevent the destruction of his beloved trees, from which his house took its name, Beaux Arbres, but succeeded only in saving the house, which had originally also lain in the direct path of the autoroute. The trees would have to fall.

He couldn't bear to witness this butchery, and decided to go away while it was taking place, but he dared not leave the house empty in his absence as it was full of treasures and objets d'arts, which might disappear if, as he feared, the workers on the autoroute broke in. This was why he needed to find a caretaker.

This was our lifeline. If he would only choose us to look after his house, it would mean that the children and I need not go back home to England. But Caroline warned us not to pin all our hopes on this because there was a possibility that two old friends of Monsieur Colombe might come to look after his house, in which case we would not be required.

We had an appointment to go and see Monsieur Colombe at his house a few days after our return from the Riviera, when we understood he would look us over and decide whether we would be suitable caretakers for Beaux Arbres during his absence. When the day arrived we drove nervously up the long straight drive, flanked by magnificent oak trees, to the fine old stone house, hardly daring to hope it might be our home for the next few months.

Monsieur Colombe came shambling out to meet us as we drove into a level semi-circular clearing in the trees behind the house. He was a man in his sixties, his tall shabbily dressed figure slightly stooped, his piercing blue eyes looking rather sternly at us under his heavy brows as we trooped into the house. He showed us into a large sitting room where we sat at a circular mahogany table and he poured us tea in blue and white willow pattern teacups and saucers. He explained that he had been left in the lurch by his two old friends whom he had hoped might possibly have come out from England to live in the house over the winter, but one of them, the wife, was ill and they couldn't come after all.

We felt his eyes on us. We could imagine what he was thinking. Could he trust us? We were, after all, complete strangers. What about the children? He eyed the girls warily. Luckily both of the girls were angelic that afternoon. They had been warned that much depended on their good behaviour and they were trying really hard. There was one tricky moment when a small glass marble escaped from Alison's grasp and rolled across the carpet towards Monsieur Colombe. We held our breath. He picked up the marble, looked across the room at Alison with the suggestion of a twinkle in his eyes and rolled it back to her. Alison picked up the marble and suddenly the moment of decision was over. We had passed the test. Monsieur Colombe told us we could move into his house the following Saturday, the day he was due to fly to New Zealand.

We promised to look after Pele, Monsieur Colombe's big white shaggy dog. Pele, presumably named after the great Brazilian footballer, was a Pyrenean mountain dog and was an instant hit with Katharine, who had always wanted a dog of her own. We followed our host into the kitchen where he showed us how to mix the dried dog food with apple peel and cores, which Pele apparently relished.

In the kitchen, Monsieur Colombe showed us an ancient pump handle, which had to be used to pump drinking water from an outside well into the kitchen sink.

Suddenly he fixed his gaze on me, and asked me never to wash my hair in the bathroom wash hand basin, as the long hairs would block up the ancient plumbing. If this happened, he warned us, French plumbers were very expensive, which explained why they always lived in the best houses in the town!

With this warning ringing in our ears, Monsieur Colombe then showed us around the house, through the sitting room once again and into the front hall, with its heavy oak double doors which were never used in all the time we were in the house.

From the hallway an elegant curved stone stairway with a cast iron balustrade swept up to the first floor. Here, as in the sitting room, we remarked on the decorative plasterwork of white Cupids and flowers on the pale pink walls. Monsieur Colombe explained that the house, which he described as a 'Folie', had been built in the eighteenth century by a rich businessman for his mistress – hence the amorous theme in the decor. The businessman kept his mistress discreetly out of the way in this house in the country, while he lived with his wife and children in the family house in Aix.

Halfway upstairs we passed a door to a spare bedroom

which Monsieur Colombe asked us not to use as, he warned darkly, there were problems with the plumbing to the wash hand basin in there.

On the first floor we discovered that the bathroom could only be reached by going through a rather shadowy room, which he told us had been his wife's bedroom. This, he said, must not be disturbed in any way. Adjoining this room, through yet another door, was his own bedroom, which we would also leave undisturbed.

He suggested that we sleep in the two remaining bed-rooms beyond his room, at the far end of the corridor. These were both double bedrooms, heavily over-furnished, but south facing and sunny, overlooking the gardens at the back of the house. To us, after our recent cramped accommodation, they seemed palatial.

At the west end of the house, accessible only through a locked outside door, was Monsieur Colombe's studio. He briefly showed us inside this large room, where we glimpsed a half-finished painting still on the easel and countless canvases stacked around the walls. The oil central heating boiler for the house was in the corner of the studio and we would need to gain entrance only to adjust the heating. Otherwise, Monsieur Colombe asked us to keep the studio locked and shuttered during his absence.

Throughout the house were many leafy indoor plants, which we promised to look after and keep well watered. On the other hand the garden outside would need little attention in these winter months.

Monsieur Colombe asked us to pay the wages of his cleaning woman, Madame Roland, who would continue to come twice a week as usual to clean the house. We readily agreed to this request and also agreed to pay for our use of the telephone, coal and wood for the open fireplace in the sitting room, and oil for the central heating. Otherwise, he said, he did not want any payment from us. We would repay him by staying at Beaux Arbres and looking after the house and contents at a sensitive time. He was concerned that his home was seen to be occupied while work was going on in the construction of the motorway so close to his house.

Amongst the contents of the house which we were to guard were many paintings, most of them by Monsieur Colombe, who was an accomplished artist, and some by his friends and fellow artists. Notably amongst these was a sketch by Pisarro, and amongst the many sculptures there was one by Matthew Smith, who with Henry Moore, had been a contemporary and colleague of Monsieur Colombe.

On the mantelpiece above the fire, reflected in the huge gilt-framed mirror was an exquisite ormulu clock and two fine vases. The antique furniture included a mahogany circular table which I instantly fell in love with and many other side tables holding objets d'arts which I resolved to put out of harm's way once we moved in.

But for Richard and me, best of all were the bookcases, holding a treasure house of volumes, both French and English, the latter promising hours of pleasure in the months to come in this incredible house. What bliss was in store for us!

With thoughts like these whirling in our minds, we could hardly contain our excitement, and I had an almost irresistible urge to hug our benefactor, but I didn't dare. He certainly had saved me from an ignominious return home, less than half way through our year, and with our house let, I would have had to find somewhere to stay for the next six months with the children. We could have gone to live with my mother, I suppose, but now that we had been given this splendid house to live in for the rest of the winter, the problem no longer existed.

As Monsieur Colombe was leaving for New Zealand only a few days into the New Year, he suggested that we move into Beaux Arbres the day following his departure. All was now fixed and we took our leave of our benefactor, wishing him 'Bon Voyage', thanking him for letting us have his home, and assuring him that we would do our best to look after it.

He brushed away our thanks. 'Just remember what I said about the plumbing,' was his parting shot.'

Jubilantly we returned to the campsite, and the cottage, another world it seemed from the beautiful house we were going to live in. It was almost like one of the stories we read each night to the girls, where all the heroine's problems are magically solved by a Fairy Godmother – or in this case a Fairy Godfather. But it wasn't a Fairy story. It was really going to happen to us, and it meant that we could all stay together and enjoy the rest of our wonderful year in France.

Over the next couple of weeks the days ticked by slowly as we packed up our caravan once again and prepared for the coming move. To all of us, impatient now to be on our way, time seemed almost to stand still, but when at last the appointed day arrived, we thankfully vacated our little cottage, said our Goodbyes or rather 'Au Revoirs' to the Dubois family and our envious friends at Camping Cezanne, promising to return to the campsite in the balmier days of summer. We issued invitations lavishly to Marie and Roger and the few hardy students remaining at Camping Cezanne as with barely concealed delight we drove away, pulling the caravan packed with bag and baggage, to our new home.

CHAPTER NINE

BEAUX ARBRES

Beaux Arbres was only a few kilometres south of Aix, not far from the village of Vauvenargues, where Picasso had bought a huge mansion, although he rarely lived there. But who cared? We had our very own mansion and we were utterly enchanted with it. As we drove up the long avenue, pulling the heavy caravan behind us, we imagined we were driving up to Manderley, and we tried to remember that wonderful description from Daphne du Maurier's superb novel 'Rebecca'.

The trees were spectacular, even in their winter skeleton outlines, and we felt sad as we looked up at the splendid oaks and the other trees which were to face such a cruel fate in the near future.

Then through the trees we saw Beaux Arbres standing majestically on the brow of the hill, and all thoughts of the trees and their sad fate left us as we followed the avenue up to the house, side-tracked the rather gloomy path which led through the north facing garden to the massive front door, and drove round into the sunny south-facing clearing at the back of the house. This time we had come to stay.

Our possessions, once unpacked from the caravan, were soon swallowed up in the kitchen and bedrooms of the house and while Richard parked the caravan under the tall pine trees at one side of the clearing, I prepared a picnic lunch which we ate at the table outside in the sunny garden. Then it was time to explore.

The land fell away in nearly all directions, rising only through the olive groves on land belonging to Beaux Arbres, to the south-east of the house. An ancient vineyard and an apricot orchard stretched from the edge of the Beaux Arbres land towards a distant farmhouse over to the

south-west, too far away to impinge on our privacy.

No other houses could be seen from the south side of the house, and although there were one or two small cottages on the roadside leading onward from the entrance to the long Beaux Arbres avenue, we could not see these even from the upstairs windows, because of the height of the trees around the front of the house. Beaux Arbres was secluded and utterly private, a situation that we relished after living in our little cottage at the campsite with people dropping in at all times of the day. That had been fun, of course, and we had all enjoyed meeting so many people, both French and English, but it was exciting to find ourselves at last in the glorious isolation and utter peace of Beaux Arbres. In any case, our friends were only a few kilometres away in Aix and we were to derive great pleasure from inviting them to visit us in due course in our new home.

Meantime, although the house was centrally heated, we foraged around outside for kindling, and as the sun disappeared behind the pine trees we lit our first fire in the great sitting room fireplace. In the firelight we all sat together, savouring our first memorable evening in that lovely room. Richard read to the girls while I prepared the evening meal and then it was time to put them to bed.

The hall and staircase seemed shadowy, in spite of the electric chandelier lighting in the hallway, and the girls mounted the stairway cautiously. It was only when we opened the door to Madame Colombe's bedroom to go through to the bathroom that they suddenly seemed reluctant to enter. It was certainly a sinister room, full of shadows, the only light coming from the landing. When I walked ahead and put on the bathroom light, they ran to join me and quickly shut the bathroom door behind them as if to keep out the shadows of the bedroom beyond. Their fear of that strange room was never to subside, especially when on the dressing table they found the hairbrushes still held the grey hairs of the mysterious former occupant of the room

That first night, however, tucked up in their own bed-room, surrounded by their favourite toys and listening to me reading the story of 'Rapunzel', they soon fell asleep, exhausted by the excitement of the day

We went on exploratory walks around the immediate vicinity and made friends with the farmer at the apricot farm next door. To his delight, Richard soon discovered in the farmer, Jean Martin, a mutual interest in Rugby. When the Martins realised that we had no television at Beaux Arbres, Richard was often invited to watch Rugby Internationals in the farmhouse that winter.

The Spring Term arrived, sweeping Richard into full time study once again, and my lessons at the Institut resumed. We were now too far out of town for Katharine to attend Maternelle, much to the regret of Madame Mesurier, who said that Katharine's French was making rapid progress and what a pity it was to remove her at this crucial stage.

However, as Richard needed the car to get to the University, the girls and I now had no transport. In any case, just before we left Val St. Andre there had been an unfortunate incident at the Maternelle when three young bearded male teacher trainees turned up one morning to observe the class. Catching sight of Katharine, whose red hair and freckles were unusual and caused much comment in France, they zoomed in on her, kissing her in the French manner on both cheeks, exclaiming, 'Quelle Mignon'. This close encounter with three complete strangers, whose long dark hair and bristling beards suddenly came so near her face, took Katharine completely by surprise and, screaming with terror, she ran to Madame for help.

She was still upset when I collected her at home time and Madame Mesurier explained what had happened. I was not surprised therefore when Katharine cried and refused to go to Maternelle next morning. I did not insist that she should go, knowing that we would soon be moving house and she would have to leave the school anyway.

Madame Mesurier was disappointed to lose her colour-ful 'petite Anglaise' and urged me to find another Maternelle for Katharine, nearer Beaux Arbres, but with-out a car this proved impossible to organise. In any case, now that we were living in such an isolated place, Alison had no other children to play with and she really needed her big sister to keep her company. With no easy alterna-tive, therefore, I settled back into having Katharine at home again. It was a relief not to have to get the girls up so early to rush out for Katharine's nine o'clock start at the Maternelle. Now they could relax. Most days they weren't going anywhere. They were quite happy to stay home at Beaux Arbres, playing for hours in the house when the weather confined them indoors, or on milder days in the garden or in the caravan which once again resumed its role as a ready made Wendy house.

Richard was usually home from the University in the late afternoon, when his first job was to light the fire. As the winter cold intensified we took great pleasure in building up a roaring fire each evening and after supper the girls would huddle up to the fire in their pyjamas and warm dressing gowns to listen to one of us read to them

Later, when they were asleep, and Richard busy at the table with his studies, I would settle down in the most comfortable armchair with a book from Monsieur Dubois' bookcase, and in this way I read my way through a prodi-gious number of wonderful novels and biographies.

One evening Richard was very late getting back from the University. He had warned me that he might be held up, but long past his usual time there was still no sign of him. By six o'clock I had lit the fire and given the girls their supper and, expecting him to burst through the door any minute the girls huddled close to me on the sofa while I read to them the nightly instalment of 'The Pudding Tree'.

Meantime, the shutters on the high windows, which I had forgotten to close, began to rattle and bang omi-nously, as the wind, which had been rising during the afternoon, grew wilder and noisier. Suddenly there was a flash followed by a resounding growl of thunder, which seemed to explode right over the house. The girls cuddled closer to me, shivering with nervous giggles as the storm intensified. As their story drew to an end, they looked beseechingly at me, hoping to put off the moment when they would have to go to bed but I hardened my heart and, closing the book firmly, I steered the two little girls reluctantly upstairs.

As we moved through Madame Colombe's shadowy bedroom to the bathroom, the lightning lit up the windows eerily and the thunder grew more violent by the minute, appearing to shake the very foundations of the ancient house, one explosion following another in quick succession. Up on the first floor the wind seemed to whine more loudly through the tall pines and lash the olive grove more madly into a flurry of noise and movement. Now the windows were under attack, shuddering as the wind tore at them as if trying to get in. I could no longer ignore the rattling of the shutters, some of which were loose and banging violently to and fro.

While the girls cleaned their teeth, I gritted mine and leaned out of the bathroom window into the screaming darkness of the night and pulled the shutters together, pulling down the cross bar into its slot inside to fix them in place.

Next it was the turn of the shutters in Madame Colombe's room. Half expecting a ghostly hand to grip mine as I leaned out of the window to close the shutters, I had to tell myself not to be so silly. This was not 'Wuthering Heights'. Madame Colombe was not Kathy. Nevertheless, I was glad to fasten the shutters of her room and then close the windows firmly against the storm. After that ordeal the task became easier. The girls followed me to their bedroom and watched as I closed the shutters on their windows.

When they were in their pyjamas I tucked them into bed, turned out the light and, leaving the door open to let in the landing light, I proceeded to close the shutters in the room beyond, where Richard and I slept. By the time this had been done, the girls were out of bed again, begging to come downstairs. They were too frightened on their own in bed that night in that spooky house, they said, and this time I couldn't refuse them. In any case, although I didn't tell them this, I was as glad of their company as they were of mine on such a night.

So we all three of us hurried downstairs once again to the warm sitting room, the girls now cosy in their dressing gowns, scampering to find their story-books. But before we could sit down and resume our reading there was one more task to do, which I was not looking forward to.

'I must go outside to close the downstairs shutters,' I reminded the girls, with more courage than I felt, for if it was a scary house inside, it was even more so outside in the dark in such a storm. By now heavy drops of rain were splashing against the windows as I put on my wellingtons and pulled the hood of my anorak tight around my head.

Then, having settled the girls together on the sofa with their books, I went out into the inky darkness, lit up intermittently by flashes of lightning. Buffeted from window to window along the house wall, I struggled as with a fiend against the wind as it tried to wrest each trembling shutter from my grasp until, at last, all the windows were barred and shuttered against the storm

The dreaded task now complete, I hurried back inside the house, locked the door, and pulled off my dripping outer clothes. Back in the cosy sitting room, while I warmed my wet hands and face by the fire, Katharine found me a towel and carefully wiped me dry. Both girls were feeling better now that we were shuttered and bolted against the storm and all the noises and terrors of the night.

How glad we all were when at last we heard a pounding on the back door, accompanied by Richard's voice, shouting 'Lct mc in! ' We all rushed to unlock the door and the ecstatic welcome he received from his three 'girls' surprised and delighted him. He was wet through, and as he dried himself, he told us that the wind had blown a tree over the road more than a kilometre away from the house. He had had to abandon the car and walk the rest of the way to the house through the darkness and the storm.

Reassured that all was safe again now that their father was here to protect them, the girls allowed Richard to put them to bed, and as I went to the kitchen to heat up our dinner I could hear them, as they went upstairs, excitedly telling their father all the scary details of the evening we had just endured.

After a hot shower Richard sat down to his dinner, and laughed at our fears. However. I think he quite enjoyed the role of being our protector, and only gently pulled my leg about letting my imagination get the better of me.

Beaux Arbres

Author with students, Katharine and Alison

Katharine and Alison at Beaux Arbres

Richard, Katharine and Alison with Pélé at Beaux Arbres

Richard with Katharine and Alison

Richard in the Basses Alpes

Hugo in the Basses Alpes

Alison with the author

Richard with workmen felling trees at Beaux Arbres

CHAPTER EIGHT

MIMI

Before he left, Monsieur Colombe had warned us that we would probably have frequent visits from a neighbour he called Mimi.

'Mimi ' he declared, 'is a sweetie, – but watch her! ' He paused before going on to explain. 'On no account let her use the telephone. She'll have no scruples about telephoning her ex-husband and various friends in Paris and Spain and all over the place. Be warned. If you're not very firm with her, you'll find yourselves footing the bill for her long-distance phone calls.'

We promised to beware of Mimi and her expensive telephone habits. We were not entirely taken by surprise therefore when, one evening shortly after we moved into Beaux Arbres, we heard the growl of a motor bike growing louder as it approached the house and then the slowing 'phut phut' as it stopped. We went to the door in time to see a petite figure wearing a huge helmet, long leather boots, a leather jacket and – incongruously – a tartan miniskirt and scarf, in process of dismounting from a large and powerful motor bike.

'Bonsoir!' she called, unbuckling her helmet as she turned towards us.

'Bonsoir Monsieur! Bonsoir Madame! Enchanté de faire votre connaissance.' Suddenly her arms were around us and we were being kissed on each cheek by this bizarre figure, helmet now removed to reveal a vivid, rather cheeky face under a mop of curly dark hair.

In rapid French she introduced herself. It was, indeed it could only have been, the famous Mimi. Inside the house, she made a bee-line for the sitting room fire and, standing in front of it, blatantly warming her backside, she explained that she lived nearby in a magnificent house,

the Mas Marat, to which as friends of her neighbour 'Arry', we were welcome at any time.

She proceeded cheerfully to quiz us about our background and our reasons for being here in France, and how we came to know 'Arry'.

In exchange she told us that she lived alone in the Mas Marat, having separated amicably from her husband, a poet, because she refused to live in Paris where he now had a separate home with their nine-year old son, who rejoiced in the name Gervaise.

'Gervaise,' she declared with typical modesty, 'is an infant prodigy. Oh, and would you mind if I make a brief phone call, just to speak to my darling boy. I miss him so dreadfully!'

Well, how could we refuse? In any case she was already on the phone and, while Richard kept a wary eye on the clock, she talked volubly in rapid French for at least ten minutes. When she returned to her place in front of the fire, she continued talking for some time about Gervaise and how wonderful he was, but there was not a word about payment for the call. She left shortly afterwards, promising to invite us to her house very soon.

Before that invitation arrived, however, she became a frequent and welcome visitor, always turning up unannounced in a whirl of noise and excitement. We found her endlessly entertaining, and a mine of information on all that we needed – or didn't need – to know about all sorts of things. She advised us, for instance, to go to the local Vinicole, or Wine Co-operative, to fill up the demi-johns with locally produced wine which was excellent, she assured us, and would cost a fraction of the price charged for the same wine in the supermarkets.

So we looked around and in the cupboard under the stairs in Beaux Arbres we found two large glass demi-johns which we loaded in the back of the car to have them filled up, one with red wine, the other with white, as Mimi had suggested.

When we arrived at the Co-Op, the first person we saw was Mimi, driving a battered Citroen 'deux cheveaux', crammed with young men, whom she had not previously mentioned, but whom she introduced with a casual wave of her hand as 'mes etudiants'. When we visited her we found that the many rooms in her vast house were rented by young male students from the University. Life in the Mas Marat, as we were to discover, was bohemian, to say the least.

Mimi, a true child of the sixties, lived her life the way she wanted and cared little what other people thought or said about her. But Mimi was also a terrible gossip, and without any prompting she told us everything about 'Arry.

On the mantelpiece above the fireplace there were two photographs in silver frames which puzzled us. One was of a young woman in her thirties, slim, blonde and very attractive. She was wearing a black swimsuit and the camera had caught her looking over her right shoulder and holding out her hand to a small curly haired girl as they climbed up a grassy bank. Who was this beautiful woman, we wondered, and who was the lady in the second photograph? This was a studio photograph of a grey haired old woman, also dressed in black, with an expression of profound sadness on her face.

Mimi told us the two photographs were of the same person, Madame Colombe. What's more, only fifteen years separated the two photographs. We could hardly believe it. How could the woman who had lived in this lovely place, who had once occupied that strange bedroom upstairs, age so quickly?

Eventually Mimi told us the story, the tragedy of Madame Colombe, indeed the tragedy of Beaux Arbres, for the house had played its part in the story.

The mysterious Madame Colombe, we learned, was Swiss, a renowned beauty from an aristocratic family when she married Harry Colombe, a man much older that herself. They had one child, Véronique, the little girl in the first photograph on the mantelpiece.

Initially happy, the marriage moved into troubled waters when, shortly after her child was born, Madame Colombe discovered that her husband was having an affair. It was one of many that were to follow in the years ahead. They came from different worlds, and behaviour which was considered acceptable in Harry's artistic milieu was intolerable to a woman from her conventional background who had married for love, and expected unwavering love and fidelity from her husband.

Monsieur Colombe admired beautiful women, especially women with red hair, and when he met Madeleine Fournier, a famous singer with beautiful auburn hair, he found her irresistible. Madame Colombe was in despair when she found out that yet again her husband was having a passionate affair with another woman. What was worse, everyone else seemed to know about the affair, and the marriage seemed doomed.

At this time Monsieur Colombe met a good looking young Englishman called Edward Hanson, an Arts Student at the university, who was looking for somewhere to stay in Aix. Harry brought the student home to Beaux Arbres and presented him to his wife, hoping that by having someone else in the house he might avoid the endless arguments over their marital problems. The strategy succeeded only too well. Madame Colombe found her lodger to be a sympathetic listener. She confided in him. She poured out her anger and resentment. .. and she found consolation. She found love. Beaux Arbres was peaceful once more.

But was not only Madame Colombe who found Edward Hanson sympathetic and attractive. Her daughter, Veronique, now a very impressionable young woman of seventeen, was home on holiday from her boarding school in Switzerland when she met and fell instantly in love with the young Englishman.

Edward had been initially flattered by the attention of the beautiful lady of the house, and willingly became her lover. However, when Veronique suddenly arrived home, he found the daughter more attractive, especially as she so obviously had fallen in love with him. All at once Edward found himself in a dangerous atmosphere of a 'ménage a trois'.

The truth eventually came out, as it was bound to do, and Monsieur Colombe banished Edward from the house. All efforts by the young lovers to meet or contact one another by telephone or by letter were blocked by Monsieur Colombe and his heartbroken wife.

Madame Colombe, who had given up hope of saving her marriage to an unfaithful husband, had now lost her lover and at the same time, even more tragically, she was estranged from her daughter.

Meanwhile the holidays had come to an end and Véronique was sent back to her Swiss finishing school. From there she promptly wrote to Edward and a secret correspondence was carried on between the two young lovers for some months until the school, alerted by a warning from Madame Colombe, opened one of the letters addressed to Veronique and discovered that it was a love letter from Edward.

This was too much for Madame Colombe, whose health, never robust, now deteriorated rapidly. She seemed to lose the will to live and her mysterious illness intensified until, transformed into the image in the second photograph, she was diagnosed with a tumour on the brain and was rushed to hospital, where within a few weeks, she died

Since then, Monsieur Colombe had lived alone at Beaux Arbres, ageing and no doubt full of regret at the misfortunes, partly of his own making, which had destroyed his family life. He had very little contact with his daughter, who after her mother's death had returned to boarding school and then gone on to University in America. Veronique had returned infrequently to France and then only for short periods. Mimi had heard a rumour that she was married, and living in Paris. Nothing was heard again of Edward Hanson.

Mimi related this sad story with appropriate drama and we felt even more the unhappy ghosts that haunted the empty bedroom of Madame Colombe.

Mimi also told us the story of how her own marriage had ended. She had gone to southern Spain on holiday with 'a friend' who lived there, and on the long return journey she had fallen asleep in the train, only to wake up well beyond her destination at Aix Railway Station, where her husband was waiting impatiently for her return.

As she was well on her way through France by the time she woke up, she decided to continue the journey to Paris, where her parents lived. From there she telephoned her husband, who was so infuriated with her that he decided he could stand no more of her outrageous behaviour, and told her he was going to divorce her.

There was obviously much more to this story than Mimi was prepared to tell us and we could imagine that what he had meant by her 'outrageous behaviour' might have had something to do with the bohemian style of life at Mas Marat.

Whatever the background to the breakdown of her marriage, however naughty her behaviour, Mimi was to us an endearing, eccentric character who revelled in her independence and seemed always to be full of joie de vivre, cheerfully laughing, talking and surrounded by young friends. What a contrast Mimi's story was, compared to the tragic fate of Madame Colombe.

We received the long promised invitation to the Mas Marat after many weeks, and found this establishment to be as bizarre as its name suggested.

At the impressive entrance, huge pillars supported high wrought iron gates, now rather rusty and in need of a coat of paint. Tonight they were left open, giving access to a long avenue lined with high poplars, which led in a dead straight line to the front door of the house, about one kilometre away. As we reached the end of this long avenue, an ancient building came into full view, its facade covered in ivy, which partly obscured several of the numerous windows. Like the rest of the building, the massive studded oak doors, thrown wide to receive us, seemed to belong to another giant species compared to the tiny figure of our hostess. Totally unabashed by the incongruous scale of her house, she was perfectly at home, and rushed to meet us with her usual exuberance, her arms flung wide in greeting, then hugging the children and kissing each of us three times on the cheeks in the warmest of welcomes.

'Entrez! Entrez!' she trilled and showed us around the entrance hall and once-elegant reception rooms on either side, whose tall windows and lofty ceilings were obviously far enough out of sight to allow her to ignore the flaking paint and plaster. There was a long dining table in one of the rooms with perhaps a dozen chairs around it, but this evening we were eating in the garden where it was warmer than in those cold unheated rooms.

When the guests, who were mostly students, were all assembled, Mimi assigned each of us different tasks. Some of the students fetched and erected trestle tables, which others covered with long white sheets. I followed Mimi to the kitchen where she told me to count out knives, forks and spoons for the ten guests, and the girls helped me carry these out and set them at places on the trestle tables. Plates, glasses and bottles appeared, carried by the students, who poured out glasses of beer and wine. Mimi, having assured herself that everyone had something to drink, disappeared into the kitchen, where she was cooking a huge paella in a pan on a scale to equal the rest of her household.

She had to be helped to carry out the heaped paella pan to the hungry guests, who had been drinking steadily in the meantime and were in excellent spirits.

The paella, accompanied by lots of crisp French bread, and washed down with more wine and beer, was excellent. The conversation was animated, the company informal and amusing and the setting incomparable. Such was the hospitality at Mas Marat.

CHAPTER NINE

PELE DISAPPEARS

Over the months we spent in Aix there were, of course, many other memorable occasions when we were invited to the homes of friends for dinner parties. We were only too aware that it would not be easy to return these invitations once we returned to the outdoor life in the caravan, so while we were at Beaux Arbres we took the opportunity of entertaining Mimi and the many other French friends who had made us so welcome in their homes. Of course we were always happy to see the young fellow students from York on less formal occasions, and there were also several mature students of various nationalities, who with their families were frequent and welcome visitors. It was a very busy social life.

One morning we received a telephone call from a Madame Courbiere, who was, she said, a cousin of Monsieur Colombe. She apologised for the short notice but said that she and her sister would like to visit us at Beaux Arbres the following afternoon. Aware that the ladies were checking up on us to see that we were not selling off the furniture or wrecking the house, I replied that we should be delighted to meet her, but once I replaced the telephone I began to panic because Pélé, Monsieur Colombe's dog, had disappeared a few days earlier, and we had no idea where he could be.

The girls and I walked as far from the house in each direction as we could, calling 'Pélé! Pélé!', but there was no answering bark, no woolly white dog bounding to meet us. Pélé had wandered off before but never for so long as this. Already worried by his long absence, we were now desperate, particularly Katharine, who missed him dreadfully and had shed many tears, certain that something awful had happened to him. In spite of my assurances to her that he would turn up, I was beginning to wonder if we would ever see him again.

When Richard came home from the university that afternoon, we set out in the car to search for Pélé at neighbouring farms and houses, but no one had seen him. Both girls cried themselves to sleep that night and I felt pretty miserable too.

Morning came, but no Pélé. I kept myself and the girls busy all morning dusting and making everything shipshape in readiness for our visitors. I also baked a chocolate cake. As it was a Saturday and Richard was free of classes, he continued the desperate search for Pélé all morning, but there was still no sign of Pélé when Madame Courbiere and her sister arrived. Both ladies were tall and thin, dressed elegantly but rather austerely in black and speaking very formal Parisian French. I showed them into the sitting room where we all sat nervously around the circular table, cleared for once of papers and books, sipping tea from Monsieur Colombe's best willow pattern tea-cups and nibbling politely at my chocolate cake. The conversation was strained. We talked about the weather, the University, Monsieur Colombe's holiday, anything under the sun except the subject uppermost in our minds, Pele.

The dreaded question came at last. Madame Courbiere set down her cup and turned to Richard to ask after the dog. 'Et the chien. Ou est Pélé– Where is Pélé?'

Suddenly we heard a scratching sound at the back door, accompanied by a familiar bark. We tried not to look too relieved, but the girls, who had up till now been on their best behaviour, were galvanised into action. Katharine left the table without even an 'Excuse me' and dashed to open the back door. Alison wordlessly followed her. Seconds later a bedraggled Pélé, his shaggy white coat several shades dirtier than usual, and emitting the most pungent smell, burst into the room.

'Oh la la!' shrieked Madame Courbiere, holding a delicate lace handkerchief to her nose. The two ladies glared in horror at the grubby Pélé who, open-mouthed and panting, his tail wagging happily, appeared to be laughing at us all. The girls, who had followed Pele into the room, were also giggling because of the delicious secret they were keeping.

'Please excuse Pélé. He's been to the farm again,' Richard apologised to the ladies. 'If you'll forgive me, Mesdames I'll take him outside, ' and so saying, he left the table and steered Pélé out of the door.

I added my apologies, explaining that Pélé sometimes went off to visit the dogs at the farm next door. The ladies appeared to accept this, laughing politely and allowing that 'Dogs will be dogs'. By this time I really didn't care what they thought about Pélé. I was so glad he was home in one piece. We could hear protesting barks outside mixed with the laughter of the girls as they helped their father shower the disreputable Pélé with the garden hose.

The ladies, having reassured themselves that the house was being cared for and that all was more or less in order, stood up and took their leave. A few minutes later they drove off, happily believing that Pélé had been gone only a matter of hours, not days.

'Phew. That was a close shave,' laughed Richard as I joined the merry circle in the garden with the freshly shampooed Pélé in their midst, innocently drying out in the afternoon sun. I could swear I saw an evil grin on his doggy face, but maybe he was just panting after his exertions.

CHAPTER TEN

A LA MONTAGNE

Pélé had accompanied us on several visits to the Basses Alpes, where we had found a ski slope within a day's journey of the house. We would set off early on a Saturday, with a picnic lunch and our skis strapped on to the roof-rack. Richard, an enthusiastic skier, would take the lift to the top of the slopes and enjoy an exciting morning's ski-ing.

Meanwhile, I was usually left with the two girls, who had their own little plastic skis, on the nursery slopes. I spent more time picking them up and re-strapping their skis than actually doing any ski-ing myself. By lunchtime when Richard returned for food, he often found me at screaming point, so after lunch he took over the children while I had my turn at the higher slopes.

Pélé, whose shaggy off-white coat was much the same colour as the snow, simply disappeared into its perfect camouflage for most of the day. All that could be seen of him now and again was his lolling pink tongue floating in space, just below two button eyes which would peer from under the fringe of curly white hair, but more often he was lost in the wide expanse of snow, happy again in his element.

At first we were alarmed, wondering if once again we had lost him, but he was obviously keeping his eye on us because somehow he always managed to re-emerge from snowy oblivion just in time for our return.

While these ski trips were very exhilarating, Richard often looked longingly at the peaks, dreaming of the chance one day of some mountaineering. At long last he met a Scotsman, Hugo Greenaway, who lectured at the University. Hugo was a bachelor, living in a luxurious apartment, driving a Sports Car and ski-ing or moun-

LES WEEKENDS AUX ALPES

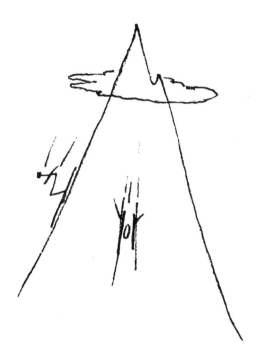

taineering each weekend in the French Alps. He spent the summer holidays sailing yachts from England out to the Mediterranean as a summer job.

Richard sometimes spent a weekend with him in the mountains, setting off before dawn to climb up high before the sun rose, and reach the summit in early afternoon, returning to base before darkness fell.

Hugo seemed to us to have an enviable life, but he confessed to Richard that it left him little time to meet any girls, and he longed to have a girl-friend with whom to share his life. Of course, we knew just the girl and introduced him to Francoise, a lovely French student whom

Richard had met in the University. Hugo and Francoise liked each other on sight, they shared common interests and soon she was his constant companion on the ski-slopes and in the mountains.

One Monday Hugo did not turn up for work, and it quickly became apparent that Francoise was also missing. A friend of Hugo's said they had gone ski-ing at the week-end in an area known to have had an avalanche.

At first we were numb with shock. To have someone we knew so well simply disappear in the snow seemed incredible. Perhaps Hugo would turn up one day, laughing at our worries. We often thought of our friend, so happy in his life, so well adjusted, especially when he found Francoise. Was that the way he would have wanted to go? Still young, active, full of plans for the future?

What about Francoise? We had introduced her to Hugo, and were so glad when the two seemed so happy together. Who could ever have foreseen that it would all end in tragedy. We could only feel very sad for both sets of parents who must feel their loss much more than any of us could imagine.

About a year later, back in England, Richard received a letter from a student friend from Aix University conveying the sad news that the bodies of Hugo and Francoise had been found in the snow where they had obviously been trapped while ski-ing in the path of an avalanche.

We looked with sorrow at the photographs Richard had taken of Hugo himself on that wonderful weekend they spent ski-ing in the Alps and cried for our dear friend, so debonair and full of life. and his lovely French girl, Francoise. They were so in love and had so much to look forward to. We spared a thought for their grieving families, who must have hoped against hope that they would both turn up one day, alive and well. How cruel fate can be.

CHAPTER ELEVEN

VISITORS FROM ENGLAND

In the February half-term friends came out from England, firstly Sarah and Lawrence Burns, with their daughter Emily, who received an ecstatic welcome from Katharine. The two were best friends back in our village in England. The Burns family had never been abroad before as a family and they had driven all the way from York in their ancient Rover.

When they recovered from what must have been a gruelling journey, we drove them around showing them all our favourite places. They loved the beautiful old town of Aix-en-Provence, with its ancient fountains and pavement cafes in the Cours Mirabeau, where we sat under colourful parasols drinking coffee.

We climbed Mont St. Victoire, Cézanne's famous mountain and visited the Museum in Cézanne's former studio in the town and later to look at Picasso's great square chateau, looming darkly over the village of Vauvenargues. Lawrence, an artist himself, was enchanted with the landscape, the light and everything he saw in this land of artists.

We made a day trip to our favourite beach on the shores of the Mediterranean at Carry le Rouet, which was also the nearest beach to Aix. West of Marseilles, this little resort did not have the cachet of beaches on the fashionable Cote d'Azur, but for that reason it was usually deserted, and we nearly always enjoyed the privilege of having the beach to ourselves when we went there with the children and sometimes one or two of the students.

We had prepared a picnic lunch and spent most of the afternoon just lazing about on the beach with the children, enjoying the sun which was really warming up during the day, although it was still early in the year.

Our friends, fresh from an English winter, enjoyed these golden days at the beach, and all the other places they visited, but most of all, Beaux Arbres worked its charm upon them. Lawrence couldn't quite believe that the sculpture so casually placed on the dining room sideboard was a real Matthew Smith, and he spent hours studying the Pisarro sketch, signed by the artist, which hung above it. He too was intrigued by Harry Colombe's paintings of ladies whose faces were forever turned away from the onlooker. 'Was there a mysterious reason behind this, or did he just not like painting faces?' he wondered. We could not answer his question. We had often wondered the same thing ourselves.

Sarah loved shopping in the colourful outdoor markets in Val St. Andre and in Aix, buying fresh fruit and vegetables for our lunch, which we sometimes ate outside at the long wooden table in the garden. As it was still rather cool in the evenings, we would eat our dinner indoors at the dining room table, the children sleepy and ready for bed after the hot days in the garden or on the beach.

One such evening, the meal just finished, we were sitting, surrounded by works of art, with the whole evening of conversation stretching ahead, when a wonderful sound drew Lawrence to the double doors. He went out quietly into the cool twilight, listened, then gestured urgently and wordlessly to us to join him. Enthralled, we stood with him in the darkness, listening to the liquid soaring song of a nightingale coming from the olive groves to the east of the house. It was the first time any of us had ever heard the nightingale's song, but there was no mistaking that beautiful sound, more enchanting than any music we had ever heard. We understood at last why Keats, Shelley and so many of the Romantic poets had been captivated by the beauty of the nightingale's song. It was an experience and an evening that none of us will ever forget.

All too soon it was time for our friends to leave but the weekend before their departure, their visit was overlapped by a couple of old friends from the University in York. Lindsay was a student in the same faculty as Richard, but one year ahead, and she was married to Bunky, who was an M.A. Student from the University of North Carolina. The couple had promised to call with us on their way home from a visit to Trepalle in Tuscany, where Lindsay's Aunt owned a vineyard and some orchards. She had a caravan permanently sited there, in which they had stayed during the previous week. They told us we could use if we wanted to visit Pisa and Florence, which were not far away from the little village of Trepalle.

Lindsay produced a few bottles of red wine from her aunt's vineyard which had the most magical effect on all of us that evening, loosening our tongues into what seemed to us to be brilliant conversation, and stimulating uncontrollable laughter in all of the company.
I wish I had a cellar full of such wine, and such good company always as we had around the dinner table that evening.

Next morning we said 'Bon Voyage' to Sarah and Lawrence, and the girls hugged Emily a tearful farewell. Then the Burns family were off on the long journey back toYork.

Bunky and Lindsay, who had a few more days' holiday, accompanied us to the market that afternoon to replenish our stock of fresh fruit and vegetables. Lindsay was fascinated by the colours and smells of the spices on display and spoke at length in her excellent French to the stall-holders.

Bunky had been complaining all weekend of a painful back, the legacy of his years playing American Football, and more recently Rugby, a game which he loved and into which he had thrown himself enthusiastically while studying at University in York.

When the pain became more intense we took him to our local Pharmacie in Aix where he bought some painkillers, which seemed to help. Bad back notwithstanding, he was a source of much entertainment to the girls, with whom he played tirelessly. One game they loved was his version of 'aeroplanes', holding one wrist and one ankle of each girl in turn and whizzing them round and round at great speed until dizziness forced them, in hysterics, to beg him to stop. Bunky was fun. They listened to the stories of his childhood in America with his mother Beezie, (all his family had wonderful nicknames) and he had a fund of wonderful jokes which he told in his North Carolina accent, bewitching to the girls, as indeed it was to all of us.

CHAPTER TWELVE

A L'HÔPITAL

On Monday of the following week when the visitors had all gone home and Richard had resumed his studies, the children reluctantly returned to a calmer rhythm of life. As I busied myself that morning with cleaning the bedrooms and washing the bed linen and towels, they were happily playing 'house' in our empty caravan.

I kept my eye on them as I went about my housework, but when I was hanging out sheets and towels on the line to dry in the warm wind, I noticed that there was no sound coming from the caravan. Suddenly apprehensive, I called to them and ran to the caravan. They were both there, apparently playing quietly, but they looked guilty and I sensed something was wrong. When I saw Alison trying to hide a little bottle in her hand, I suddenly felt worried.

'What have you got there, Alison?' I asked. Alison wordlessly tried to hide her hand behind her back. 'Give me that bottle!' I demanded, and reluctantly her little hand opened up and I took from it an empty bottle of Junior Aspirin.

'We were just playing Doctors and Nurses!' Katharine was crying. 'Honestly, Mummy, I told her not to eat them, but she wouldn't listen to me.'

'What!' I shouted. 'Were there some pills in this bottle? Did you eat them?'

Alison was crying now, too. Her mouth was open, and to my horror I saw that inside it her tongue was coloured orange. She must have eaten several pills.

'Where did she get these pills from? How many did she take, Katharine? How long ago...?

'Just now Mummy. It was just a little bottle. We found it up there.' She pointed at the wall cupboard. 'I'm sorry,

Mummy. I told her you'd be angry.'

'Did you eat any?' I asked Katharine, feeling sick with panic.

'No, Mummy. She ate them all.'

'Oh no!' I wailed, horror engulfing me. I scooped the now frightened Alison up in my arms and, shouting to Katharine to follow us, I ran to the telephone in the house and dialled the emergency number. Fortunately my French was just about good enough to ask for an ambulance and after explaining between my sobs what had happened, to give our address. I answered the urgent questions asked of me as well as my French would allow, and the voice told me that the ambulance would be with me directly.

Then, kissing and hugging my little Alison tightly in my arms, I waited, becoming more and more anxious by the minute as I thought of what might happen. Then, partly to make the time pass more quickly, I took the girls to the bathroom where I washed their grubby hands and tearstained faces. I rubbed the flannel over my own tearstained face and hastily combed my hair, thinking as I did so how unimportant my appearance was in the circumstances. At last through the open window we heard the Ambulance siren approaching from some distance away on the road, but then it passed and seemed to fade again in the opposite direction.

'He's missed our turning!' I cried, panic overwhelming me as I picked Alison up in my arms. 'Come on, Katharine. We'll have to run down the drive. Maybe he'll turn round and see us on the way back.'

I grabbed my handbag, and locking the door, I hurried down the drive, sometimes running, sometimes walking, with Alison growing heavier by the minute in my arms and Katharine hanging on to my other hand, as she did her best to keep up with me. Never did the drive seem so long as on that terrible day.

Luckily the ambulance driver must have realised that he had gone too far and asked for directions. He met us at the end of the drive, and minutes later we were speeding, siren sounding, along the country roads, then in the town, passing other traffic at breakneck speed until we reached the hospital. Ironically, the girls had always wanted a ride in one of these Citroen Ambulances, which often flashed past us with blue lights flashing and the siren screaming. They had their wish now, all right, but how I wished we were anywhere but here on this nightmare journey.

At last we were at the hospital and rushing with Alison into Accident and Emergency, where once again I explained to the Doctor in charge the details of what had happened.

'Where is the bottle?' asked the Doctor, and with increasing urgency, obviously thinking that I didn't understand French he said in English, 'I need the bottle which contained the pills. I need to read the label so that I understand what the child has swallowed.'

I looked at him, suddenly realising how stupid I was. In my panic I had left behind the empty aspirin bottle, which would have given him all the information that he needed. When I told him this the Doctor sighed and asked me if I knew exactly the chemical contents of the pills, but of course I only knew that they were Junior Aspirin and that as far as I knew, Alison had eaten the whole bottle full, about 20 or 30 pills in all. He muttered something in French and told me to go home again and get the bottle.

Unfortunately Richard had the car and I had therefore to tell the Doctor that I had no transport, so minutes later I found myself and Katharine once again in an Ambulance, the driver breaking all the speed limits back to Beaux Arbres to fetch the empty bottle of Aspirin. While at the house, I took a moment to write a letter of explanation to Richard, who would worry when he found no one at home.

By the time Katharine and I returned to the hospital with the bottle, the panic was over. They had pumped out Alison's stomach and she was recovering in the Children's Ward. I was ushered into the office, where the Doctor in charge of this ghastly operation wished to speak to me.

'Is she normal' the Doctor asked me bluntly.

'What do you mean?' I asked, panicking once again as my imagination seized upon all the possible implications of this question.

The Doctor told me that it had taken a couple of nurses to hold Alison down while they pumped her stomach. 'You say she is only two and a half years old,' he said 'but she is so big! Her strength is formidable – like a child of four or five.'

Was that all? I breathed again. I supposed she did seem big compared to the petite little French girls, but I assured him that she was quite normal for a child of her age in England.

'But how is Alison? Will she be all right, now? Can I take her home?' I asked him anxiously.

Now that he knew what the pills contained, he said, he was able to reassure me that my little daughter should be fine. But, he added acidly, no one but the English would be so stupid as to make dangerous medicines with a pleasant orange flavour, for children. In any case, he would need to keep her under surveillance in the hospital overnight, just in case the drugs caused any further reaction. Meantime, he summoned a nurse who would take us to see Alison.

As the Nurse took us to the Children's Ward, I felt another sharp stab of fear. The nightmare was not over yet. I hated the thought of leaving Alison alone in the unfamiliar surroundings of a hospital amongst strangers who spoke a language she couldn't understand. But when the Nurse assured me that Alison could probably go home the following morning, I had to be content with that.

When Alison saw us coming she jumped up and down in her cot, shouting 'Mummy! Mummy! ' I lifted her up and hugged her to me and sat down with her on my knee, so that Katharine could hug her too. It was wonderful to see my baby looking apparently none the worse for her ordeal. In fact she looked the picture of health in the blue cotton pyjamas which, as the nurse told me, were supposed to fit a boy of three, but were all they could find to fit her.

The nurse told us that Alison had put up a noisy resistance and generally given them a lot of trouble, until in the end they found the only person who could control her was a huge black nurse from The Cameroons, whose brilliant smile and smattering of English eventually pacified my troublesome daughter.

We refused to leave Alison until Richard arrived and then we went through the long story once again while he listened, appalled at what might have happened. He hugged and cuddled Alison who was still scared but at the same time obviously enjoying being the centre of attention, with everyone laughing and crying over her at the same time. We stayed with the patient as long as the hospital would allow, but when the time came for us to leave she started crying again and we could hear her heartbroken cries of 'Mummy! Mummy!' as we walked farther and farther away along the corridors of the hospital.

Neither Richard nor I got much sleep that night, and next morning we got up early and Richard telephoned the hospital to enquire about Alison's progress. He was told that she had had a good night's sleep and as she was no longer in danger we could come and collect her from the hospital. This was great news and we immediately set out for the hospital, arriving at Reception just after nine o'clock. There were told that we could take Alison home, but first there was the matter of payment. In the drama of all that had happened the day before, we had forgotten that the French National Health Service was quite different from our own free Health Service, insofar as you have to pay and then claim back part of the cost through your National Insurance. Now we were faced with a large bill, which we certainly couldn't pay. Fortunately, before leaving England we had been given good advice and taken out Student Insurance against accident and illness, but we needed to go home and study this before we were sure that Alison's treatment and stay overnight in a French hospital was covered under the terms of the policy.

Richard somehow persuaded them that he would return with the Insurance Policy and sort all this out later. Just now, his daughter was more important.

A feeling of utter relief washed over me as, together once again as a family of four, we hurried through the doors of the hospital, Richard carrying the precious little bundle in his arms while I followed, tightly holding Katharine's hand, as though fearful they might hold her as hostage. Thankful that Alison was safely recovered, we stowed her in the car and drove back to the safety of Beaux Arbres.

Abandoning any thought of going to lectures that day, Richard spent his time sharing the children with me, as if we had suddenly learned how precious they were to us. Later that evening, when our little girls were safely in bed, we spent some time studying the Insurance Policy, which we had taken out with a company that specifically dealt with Student Insurance. We were relieved to find that hospital treatment for all the family in European countries was covered by the policy, and we went to bed that night feeling confident that the immediate problem was solved.

In the middle of the night we were awakened by a sleepy Katharine, who came to our room in tears and wailed 'There's something wrong with Alison.'

She was right. We hurried to Alison's bedside to find her with a soaring temperature, delirious, and when we lifted her from the bed, she was violently sick. We called a Doctor, who came almost immediately and examined Alison. He asked us several questions and when we outlined Alison's recent history, he telephoned the hospital, arranged a bed for Alison and instructed us to take her to the hospital without delay.

I thanked the Doctor for coming out in the middle of the night to help us. He looked at me in scorn and said. 'Madame, you are in France. When you call a Doctor he will come. We have not your English National Health Service here!'

Somewhat abashed and by now thoroughly alarmed, we rushed once again to the hospital, and once again went through the distressing experience of being separated from Alison.

We waited while a Doctor examined her, but apart for saying that she must stay in hospital under supervision, he would not pronounce on her condition, saying that we should go home and get some sleep. He could tell us more in the morning.

After another sleepless night, we telephoned the hospital next morning. We were told that Alison was suffering from a bout of gastro-enteritis, which we secretly decided she had probably caught during her last stay at the hospital. However, she was responding well to treatment but it would be at least two or three days before they would allow her to come home.

So we returned to that awful routine again where we visited Alison each day in the hospital, each time re-enacting the distressing scenes we had already experienced when we first had to part with her, leaving her alone overnight in the hospital.

In the evenings we went with Richard, but because he had to resume his studies during the day at the University, Katharine and I kept the car and went to see Alison on our own.

One afternoon a voice on the hospital loud speaker system announced that Madame French was required at Reception. Telling Alison that I would be back soon, I hurried with Katherine to the Reception desk. There an officious young man handed me a bill for several thousand Francs, and demanded instant payment. I tried to explain that we had Insurance, but this word drove him into a fury, and banging the desk and shouting something to the effect that he wasn't interested in English Insurance Companies, which never paid up, he again demanded payment in a most menacing way. When I explained that my French was not good enough to argue but if he would permit me I would telephone my husband who would be able to explain our situation, he refused to let me go even as far as the telephone booth in the foyer.

The French people in the queue behind me were sympathetic and muttered their disgust at the official. One woman protested that he should not behave in this insensitive manner to a visitor to France, who was so obviously distressed already. Katharine looked terrified and I managed to shed a few tears, which were sincere enough, as I was genuinely afraid that he would not let us take Alison home, now that she was better.

In the end the official relented so far as to let me go away to make the telephone call, on condition I came back directly to the desk. I fled, grateful to make my escape, and when I got through to Richard, who had just arrived home, he told me on no account to return to the desk, but to drive home with Katharine, and he would come in to the hospital and face the official himself.

When Richard arrived at the reception, the official ranted at him for a while and at first refused Richard's request to see the Director of the Hospital. However, after insisting for some time that he wanted to see the Director, Richard was referred to this gentleman who listened politely to his explanation, looked carefully at the terms of the Insurance Policy and accepted it without further question. He ordered the hospital to release Alison into our care. We could take her home as soon as she was ready.

So for a second time we carried Alison though the doors, hoping and praying that it would be the last we saw of hospitals in France – as indeed it proved to be.

It was so good to have Alison home again, playing happily with Katharine, apparently none the worse for her experience, and soon the whole episode was forgotten, at least by the children. For Richard and me it remained with us throughout that year as our worst nightmare and made me even more vigilant than I had been before.

Before I allowed them back into the caravan to play, I made a thorough search of every nook and cranny in the cupboards. How could I have been so negligent before?

But the small bottle had been lying on its side, above eye-level and hidden by the frame of the cupboard. Only by climbing up on to the top of the unit below, and feeling along the bottom of the cupboard above her head, had one of the two children, and I never discovered which one, discovered the bottle, which had caused all the trouble.

Once the children were in bed that first night after Alison's return from the hospital, Richard and I emptied all the cupboards in the bathroom of bottles and cartons of medicine. We filled a large cardboard packing case with these pills and potions, many of them lethal, and hid the box on top of a wardrobe in one of the forbidden bedrooms.

Only then did we begin to feel safe again. Thank heaven the children hadn't been playing Doctors and Nurses in the bathroom.

CHAPTER THIRTEEN

IN LOCO PARENTIS

Not many weeks later Richard had to tackle the health authorities once again, but this time it was in response to an SOS call from Vivienne, one of his fellow York Students, who, after having some emergency treatment for a painful wisdom tooth at a Dental Surgery in Aix, found herself in a similar situation to our recent experience at the hospital.

Before being allowed to leave the Dental Surgery she was faced by a blunt demand for a large cash payment and, in spite of producing a valid Insurance Policy, she was threatened with legal action if she refused to pay. She called us at Beaux Arbres and tearfully related her dilemma. Richard drove straight to the Dental Surgery and put his well-practiced argument into play once again. Fortunately the Dentist relented when Richard reassured him and offered to telephone the Insurers in England who would validate the claim.

Once again he brought the patient, Vivienne, back home to Beaux Arbres, looking thoroughly shaken but relieved and most grateful to Richard for getting her out of a very upsetting situation. She wasn't feeling well enough to join us for a meal, but after a cup of tea and a lot of sympathy we put her to bed until she felt better and then we took her home to sleep it off.

Some of the young students from York seemed accident prone, to say the least, and by now they had come to regard Richard as someone on whom they could call for help. One day in the Spring term we received a tearful telephone call from Ros and Anita, two of Richard's fellow students from York. They were in quite a frantic state and asked if they could come and see us as a matter of urgency. When they arrived at Beaux Arbres about an hour later, tearstained and in obvious distress, we persuaded them to sit down by the fire and try to calm themselves. Eventually, after mugs of tea they felt calmer and we settled down to hear their story.

They told us that they had been invited by some of the York Students at Lyons University to go and stay the weekend, but, having no money for the train fare, they had decided to hitch a lift to Lyons. All went well at first. They were, after all, attractive young women and had no difficulty in getting lifts. Then, just outside Valance they were picked up by a man in a Citroen who said he was going to Lyons himself. Naturally delighted, the girls jumped in to the car, Ros sitting in the front passenger seat and Anita in the back. Once on the move again, they cheerfully answered all his questions and entertained him by telling him about their year at University in Aix. They were chattering happily in this manner when suddenly they realised that without any warning he had left the main road and turned off into a side road.

Alarmed, they asked him where he was going and why he had left the main road to Lyons. Without offering a reply he carried on driving until they found themselves slowing down and turning off the road, through an open gate into a field, where the car stopped. Alarmed, the two girls hastily got out, pulling their rucksacks from the boot, when the Frenchman, a burly fellow, attacked Anita, the taller of the two girls, and after a struggle forced her to the ground with his heavy figure on top of her. There was now no possible doubt about his intentions. Ros, a slightly built girl, at first stood helplessly by, screaming with terror.

Then, pulling herself together, she cast around for some means of helping her friend. In the absence of any other weapon, she unclasped the buckle on her leather shoulder bag, wrapped the sturdy leather strap around the Frenchman's neck and, placing her foot on his back, pulled with all her strength. Nearly throttled, the Frenchman's hands reached for his throat to release the choking strap. Finding herself free of his grasp, Anita threw him off, rolled over and struggled to her feet. Before he could recover, the two girls picked up their rucksacks and ran for their lives through the open gateway and on to the road.

Their assailant, who was in no condition to stop them, passed them in his car some minutes later, shaking his fist and scowling, but the girls felt safe, as even on this minor road there was sufficient traffic to prevent him attempting to harm them further. It was doubtful that he would have had felt the inclination to tackle such resourceful young women a second time.

Thoroughly scared by this encounter, the two girls had wisely decided to abandon the trip to Lyons, instead returning to Aix, still hitching lifts, but taking care to get into cars with married couples or family parties. Fortunately, they had experienced no further misadventures and apart from the delayed shock, which had left them feeling rather hysterical, they seemed none the worse off.

We had followed their story with mounting horror at the thought of what might have happened to these two sweet girls who were usually so full of fun and laughter but had been suddenly faced with near disaster. They were still very shocked and in need of lots of comfort and reassurance, which we tried to give them. There were many hugs and tears and cups of tea, and I would not let them go home without joining us for an evening meal.

During the course of the evening we talked to them at some length about the risks they were taking in hitch hiking, and how tragically their story might have ended. As it happened, Ros had been very resourceful, and saved her friend Viv and probably herself from a terrible fate. We tried to get them to face up to the reality of what might have happened to them. They might have both been raped or even murdered. They assured us that they realised that they had been very lucky and it might easily have turned out very badly. Richard made them promise not to attempt hitch-hiking again in France, or indeed anywhere else. The risks were too great.

I could see that both girls were still very shaken and I offered to put them up overnight in the spare room. But they were beginning to feel more like themselves and said they felt ready to go back home. Promising to take more care of themselves in future, they hugged me and my girls again and waved to us as Richard drove them off home. Soon after, as I put my little girls to bed, I prayed that somehow I could keep them safe from such dangers.

It had obviously been a relief for the two girls to have someone to whom they could tell their sorry tale, and as we were the only married couple in the group of students from York, we were happy to act in loco parentis and for them to use Beaux Arbres as a refuge, a substitute for their own home in a foreign and suddenly frightening country.

As time went on we found ourselves used more and more as a shoulder to cry on when things went wrong. At times we felt a great weight of responsibility for these young people, and we were genuinely concerned that they sometimes seemed very naive, if not foolhardy. For instance, we were appalled to hear some time later that Ros and another girl had gone hitch-hiking again. It seemed that our words of warning had fallen on deaf ears. Would they never learn?

The students' own parents did come out to visit them in Aix at Easter, just before Mr. Colombe's return, and we had a big party one evening at Beaux Arbres with all nine students and several of their parents who had travelled out to Aix. Needless to say, no mention was made of the ill-fated trip to Lyons, and all the parents seemed impressed that their son or daughter had matured sufficiently to survive the year so far. Little did they know!

Beaux Arbres was the perfect setting that evening and its large elegant rooms easily absorbed the large number of guests. One of the quietest of the students was called Judith Savage. Her parents came that night and predictably were the most reticent of the guests. They stayed apart from the rest of the company, talking to their daughter, and when the food was served everyone turned up in the dining room to eat except Judith and her parents.

I called to Richard. 'Tell the Savages to come to eat. They must be hungry.'

There was much good-natured merriment among the assembled company when they heard this, and when the Savages eventually entered the room, red faced with embarrassment, they were the most unlikely looking savages anyone could imagine!

THE SAVAGES ARE HUNGRY

There were other S. O. S. calls from the York students in Aix. Viv, a lively brunette, had been taking photographs throughout her stay in Provence, but one day her hobby landed her in trouble. She had been taking shots of one of the many fountains in Aix. The three main fountains were in the Cours Mirabeau, but that morning she found a secluded Square, in the centre of which was a fountain coursing out of the mouth of three dolphins. She had been snapping this fountain from various angles when she suddenly found herself surrounded by several Gendarme officers, bristling with guns, who hustled her inside the nearest police station and proceeded to question her about her reasons for being in Aix, and in particular why she was photographing the buildings in the Place du Dauphin. In vain did she protest that her interest was in the fountain and not the buildings behind it. They did not believe her, but after a couple of hours of relentless questioning they allowed her to make one phone call.

She telephoned Beaux Arbres and, obviously very distressed, begged us to come and get her out of the clutches of the law. So Richard once again went to the rescue and somehow persuaded the Gendarmerie that Viv was indeed an enthusiastic photographer and not a spy or a terrorist.

They were hard to convince that she was not a member of the 'Red Brigade' or any of the other militant student movements involved in the 1968/9 student riots which had convulsed Paris and the rest of France throughout 1968, and were still causing considerable trouble throughout our time in Aix which followed shortly afterwards.

We sometimes visited the students in their rented rooms in various parts of the town. Viv and Ros shared a room in a fine villa, newly built by the owners, Monsieur Sagan and his wife. Like many French houses, it was hidden behind high fences, with massive wrought iron gates, which were opened only at the command of someone inside the house. Even then, we were faced with two fierce Doberman Pincher dogs straight out of 'The Hound of the

Baskervilles' who lunged at the gates, snarling and slavering to get at our throats. Unwilling to get any closer to these two monsters, we waited outside until Madame Sagan came out to assure us that her dogs would not harm us. Unconvinced, we edged through the gates, ready to flee at any moment, but with Madame's protection the dogs allowed us to walk unscathed to the door.

Inside, we were shown around the beautiful house, of which Madame Sagan was justly proud. The two English girls shared a large pleasant bedroom with two single beds and a lovely view from the window. They were treated as members of the family, and shared the family dinner each evening. As Madame Sagan spent hours in the kitchen each day preparing a wonderful meal for her husband, they considered themselves very fortunate.

How astonished they were, therefore, when they returned one day from the University to find Madame Sagan, her head on her arms, seated at the kitchen table sobbing uncontrollably. She raised a tearstained face to look at them. Her husband, she wailed, had left her for a younger woman. She, who had spent her days making his home perfect, shopping and cooking for hours each day so that he would have a delicious meal each evening – she had been abandoned in the home that they had built together.

She was inconsolable, and Viv and Ros were distressed for her, disgusted with Monsieur Sagan and unable to understand how he could so callously desert the wife who adored him and who had devoted her life to making him comfortable and happy. But in France, as everywhere else in the world it was ever thus, or as the French say, 'C'est la vie'.

Ros, blonde, lovely Ros, had many admirers among the French male students, but her current boyfriend was a young man whom we had seen loitering in the vicinity of her lodgings, wearing a white trench coat, a trilby hat and dark glasses, looking for all the world like a member of the Mafia. Ros had secretly told us, amid great hilarity, that

Bernard as he was called, carried a stiletto tucked in his sock. He was passionately in love with her, of course, and declared himself ready to die if she would not marry him. But one day, discussing himself and his feelings, as he was very fond of doing, he declared that he could never marry a woman who had loved another man.

'Oh well!' laughed Ros gaily, 'That counts me out. I've been in love at least a dozen times before you came along.'

The love affair ended abruptly, but Ros was far from heartbroken. She had, she told us, become rather bored with her Latin lover, who after all loved himself more than he loved her or anyone else and who lacked that one quality which so endeared us to Ros – a sense of humour. Bernard was ever afterwards referred to by Ros as 'Bernardo, mio Mafioso'.

A rather more serious problem arose for all the students, including ourselves, during the Post Office Strike in Britain which lasted about three months during the Spring of 1971. Among all the other letters held up were the all-important Student Grant cheques, which were our only source of funds.

Fortunately for us, we had arranged with our bank in York to issue us with an EC Bank Card to access our Bank account in England while we were in France. We continued to use this card throughout the three months of the strike, even though we knew that there was no money left in our account.

For this purpose we made many visits to the Cours Mirabeau where all those impressive buildings we had earlier admired included several Banks. Richard and I took great care to use a different Bank each time we used our EC Bank Card to cash money. We also took turns in going in to cash the equivalent of thirty pounds, about three hundred Francs, which was our cash limit, and which kept us going for about a week at a time. We were always afraid that the officials in the Banks would recognise us and realise that we had been using the card continuously over several months. We also half expected that our Bank

Manager at home would by some means block our card. The EC Bank card was designed for tourists to use on holiday for a few weeks, and not for students to use to survive on for several months against a background of a mounting overdraft in their home bank. Somehow, we survived and that magical little plastic card kept us eating until the emergency was over.

When, about three months later, the strike ended we received, along with all the other mail, a heap of letters from our Bank Manager in York telling us with increasing insistence that we could not have any more money. Fortunately we also received two grant cheques which had also been held up, and which we cashed and lived on for many weeks, thus giving our beloved Bank card a well earned rest.

The other York students, who had no cash cards, were left penniless in France, their grant cheques held up in England for the duration of the strike, and while we were able to help to feed them at first, they realised we couldn't continue to support them on our mounting overdraft, and one by one they were forced to go back home to borrow money from their parents until the emergency was over.

I remember producing a huge pot of stew at this time for the nine York students in Aix and a few of the York students who had come down from Lyons University to visit us. One young man from Lyons regarded the food on his plate hungrily, but before tucking in he looked at me and enquired ingenuously 'Is this horsemeat?'

I was very offended at first, but on reflection I had to admit that it was not such an unreasonable assumption, as by then some of them were literally hungry enough to 'eat a horse' – and anyway the French apparently enjoyed doing just that, and had special butchers shops 'Chevaleries' which sold only horsemeat. However, we were never tempted to break this English taboo by eating the meat of the horse

CHAPTER FOURTEEN

Timber!

The building of the Autoroute was proceeding apace, and in the evenings we often walked down the long drive from Beaux Arbres to the scene of devastation from which Monsieur Colombe had decided to escape.

His beautiful cedar and many fine oak trees had indeed been felled. We felt great sadness, even as we marvelled at the huge circumference of the trunks and took photographs of these felled giants, with Richard standing beside them to show their stature, measured against the height of a man.

The workmen who had felled the trees were friendly enough. They had their job to do, but assured us that they took no pleasure in cutting down such magnificent trees, and when we explained how Monsieur Colombe felt about his oaks, they posed for photographs beside the upturned trunks. They also agreed to cut several rounds from the trunks to leave for Monsieur Colombe, if he so wished, to have splendid solid circular oak tables made from them. To Richard they offered the branches for firewood to feed the hungry fire in the Beaux Arbres fireplace through the winter. He spent many evenings and weekends sawing and chopping at the branches until he had a great store of firewood neatly stacked. How we enjoyed those fires roaring up the chimney while we read our books or entertained our friends who came to warm themselves at the Beaux Arbres hearth that winter.

We watched the workmen demolish a neighbouring farmhouse, in which a few weeks earlier a whole family had lived, and we learned that, had Monsieur Colombe not fought and won a campaign to save his home, Beaux Arbres itself would have gone under the motorway soil as the bulldozers tore their relentless way south. We suddenly realised what a fight he must have put up, and how despairing he must have felt at losing so much of his land and his magnificent trees.

He would certainly have hated seeing the motorway gouging its merciless scar of earth through the serene countryside so close to his home. We felt something of his despair as day after day that spring we saw yet more magnificent trees and vegetation fall victim to the insatiable appetite of the bulldozers.

One evening, however, on our daily pilgrimage to the scene of devastation below the house, we were astonished and delighted to find the earthy autoroute corridor entirely covered in brightly coloured tulips. Flaming scarlet, pretty pink and brilliant yellow, they had pushed through the convulsion of brown earth in a floral demonstration of defiance against the invading monsters, and made the whole area a scene of unexpected colour and beauty. Where had the tulips come from? Perhaps the little farmhouse garden had once had a bed of tulips, which now took their last chance to bloom before the tarmac buried them forever. We never knew, but gratefully filled our arms with them, and for days the sunny rooms of Beaux Arbres overflowed with this unexpected bounty from the desecration that the motorway left in its wake.

As Easter approached, we prepared ourselves for the return of Monsieur Colombe. The weather was much warmer now, and surprisingly I found myself really looking forward to our return to the caravan. Beaux Arbres had been a godsend in the cold months of winter and we had revelled in its elegance and its spacious rooms while we were confined indoors by the weather. We had certainly enjoyed reading all Mr. Colombe's English books in comfortable chairs by those lovely log fires, but now that the spring had returned, I found myself becoming impatient with the endless housework. The responsibility of looking after someone else's home, however fine, had been at times a heavy one and I longed for the carefree gypsy life we had tasted for a few brief months the previous autumn.

The girls too were keen to return to the campsite, with its inexhaustible supply of little friends to play with at the swings and the swimming pool. They loved the intimacy of the caravan where they were not sent upstairs to a remote bedroom but went to sleep in their cosy bed behind the curtain listening to the murmuring of our voices, and woke up to the doll's house life that we lived in that confined space.

Perhaps Richard was the only one who did not look forward to our cramped quarters, where it must have been difficult to study, but he regarded the whole year as a marvellous adventure and adapted easily.

AU REVOIR TO BEAUX ARBRES

The day came when Monsieur Colombe returned home. In the midst of all our packing and preparations to leave the house, I had prepared a meal for all of us to share before we left. As we sat around the table he told us about his holiday in New Zealand. He was disappointed because he said, New Zealand was very like Switzerland, where he had spent most of his life, and he hadn't really enjoyed being there.

He asked about the house and we told him how much we had come to love living in Beaux Arbres, and how comfortable and warm it had been through the bleak months of winter. We owned up to breaking a cup and saucer, and the demise of one of his beloved indoor plants, probably from over-watering, he said. He was obviously annoyed by these small losses, but he must have been relieved that nothing major had gone wrong.

Richard asked if there was anything we could do to help him, now that he was home again, such as gardening or chopping wood. Monsieur Colombe looked meaningfully at me with his piercing eyes under those grey eyebrows and suddenly I knew what he was going to ask. I felt my face blush under that steady gaze and, all too aware of the fact that most of the pictures on the walls around us were nudes, I awaited his reply with dread.

'Well, now that you ask, yes, you could do something for me,' he said, never taking his eyes off my face. 'Your wife could pose for me.'

Richard, suddenly aware of the implications of this request, and obviously unable to think of a reasonable way of refusing, was speechless.

'Yes, of course. I would be glad to pose for you, Monsieur Colombe,' I replied.

'What else could I say, in the circumstances?' I protested later to an irate husband, as we trundled down the drive from Beaux Arbres towing the caravan with all our possessions packed hastily inside. Our stay in that lovely house was over, but somehow the feelings we should have had about leaving Beaux Arbres were overshadowed by this silly argument about my posing for Monsieur Colombe.

We had tried to express our gratitude to our benefactor for everything he had done for us, but he had in his usual manner brushed away our thanks, after making an appointment with me for a sitting the following week.

'Anyway, he didn't say anything about posing nude,' I reminded Richard.

Richard wasn't convinced, however, especially as Monsieur Colombe had expressly asked that I come alone, as he did not want any distractions while he was painting.

We settled back into Camping Cezanne and by the time the dreaded day of the sitting arrived, Richard had devised an elaborate system by which he would telephone Beaux Arbres some time after I arrived, asking to speak to me, and if I had been asked to undress, I would give him a coded message in whatever I said, and he, Richard, would come to my rescue. How ridiculous!

Fortunately, Mr. Colombe merely asked me to sit, fully clothed, in a comfortable chair, without moving, and when the telephone rang, to his utter fury, he held it out to me, barely disguising his impatience as I spoke to my anxious husband and put his mind to rest, in code as arranged.

'I hope he's not going to keep interrupting like this,' said Mr. Colombe querulously when I had put the phone down and solemnly resumed my pose. I suddenly had an irresistable urge to laugh when I thought of the ridiculous plan we had devised. My shoulders, my whole body shook and my face crumpled. It was all I could do not to burst into loud uncontrollable laughter. I'm sure he knew very well what was bothering Richard, because he later informed us that he mentally undressed all the women who modelled for him, because of this tiresome unwillingness of many of the ladies of his acquaintance to pose in the nude.

We got to know Monsieur Colombe much better during the next few months and became less in awe of him. On one occasion he invited us to Beaux Arbres to meet a lady friend of his who was visiting him from England. Marion was a charming woman, now a widow, whose husband had been a diplomat. She had obviously been used to living in exotic surroundings in various British Embassies abroad, but had now retired to a house in rural Sussex. She confided in me that Harry had asked her to marry him but she was unsure about whether or not she really wanted to live in Beaux Arbres. Wasn't it rather isolated? What did I think? She was, she said, used to her own pattern of life in Sussex, with a circle of friends with whom she played Bridge. She didn't drive and she wondered if Harry would want to take her in to Aix for her weekly hairdressing appointment, and for shopping trips and so on. What was it like to live in Beaux Arbres? Wasn't it very isolated? What about the winter?

I tried to reassure her about Beaux Arbres, but at the back of my mind was that stormy night with the wind howling in the olive groves and the shutters banging all over the house. I couldn't help wondering if she would sometimes find it just as eerie as we had done, and would she feel the brooding presence of the first Madame Colombe in that strange bedroom? I said nothing about all this, however, and gave a generally rosy picture of life in Beaux Arbres, but I could not imagine that Harry would take kindly to shopping trips when he had work in hand.

We heard later from Harry that she had turned down his proposal of marriage, preferring to maintain their friendship at a distance, with a visit from time to time. I felt sorry for Harry and I secretly hoped that she had not been put off by anything that I had said. Thinking about it now, I'm sure she could read the situation. She was no fool and in any case she had been very hesitant and unsure about the proposal from the outset, so that her decision was not unexpected.

When, years later, we took our teenage girls back to revisit the scenes of their childhood year in France, Monsieur Colombe was still living alone in Beaux Arbres, an old man now, still grumbling away, still painting. As he said of himself, 'I'm well over eighty – quite ga-ga you know. I don't know what I'm doing here, still plodding along. I should have died years ago.' He didn't seem in the least ga-ga to us. Those piercing eyes were still very much aware of what was going on.

Katharine and Alison

Katharine in the apricot orchard at Beaux Arbres

The Author with Pélé in the kitchen at Beaux Arbres

The Author with Richard, a friend and Pélé at Beaux Arbres

Richard, Katharine and Alison on the pond
at Camping Cézanne

Katharine and Alison at Camping Cézanne

Richard in the Basses Alpes

*The Author with Karharine and Alison
in Trepalle, Italy*

The Author and Richard in the garden at Beaux Arbres

Katharine and Alison with Janet, Pascale and Jacques

The Author and girls with Janet and family
five years later

Katharine, Alison, the Author and Monsieur Colombe
ten years later

CHAPTER SIXTEEN

HOLIDAY IN ITALY

As this chapter of our lives in Beaux Arbres came to a close it was not without pleasure that we returned to the campsite in Val St. Andre, with its rustling poplar trees, its stunning view of Mont St Victoire, its swimming pool and swings, and of course, the Happy Lion water spout, which Alison and Katharine greeted like a long lost friend.

It was Easter, and Richard had a few weeks holiday from the University. We had recently received a letter from Lindsay repeating her earlier invitation to use her aunt's caravan in Trepalle, which was available for us if we wanted to go there during the Easter holidays. We bought a map of Italy on which we found Trepalle, a small village not far from Pisa and Florence, cities which I had visited on holiday with my mother nearly ten years earlier. Richard had often heard me talk of the wonders of those fabulous places with their wealth of Renaissance architecture, sculpture and art. Here was an opportunity not to be missed, and it was not difficult to persuade Richard that we must go to Trepalle, especially as this time we had a caravan already there waiting for us and we would not have to take our own caravan with us. That made the journey a great deal simpler.

Richard carefully mapped out our route, avoiding the traffic of the Riviera, which we knew would be congested at this busy holiday time. Instead of going south to the Mediterranean coast, we took a route north-eastwards through the Basses Alpes, passing over the border into Italy at the Col de Larche. It was snowing as we crossed into Italy through this high mountain pass but the temperature rose dramatically as we drove down towards Genoa.

Farther south, along the Italian Riviera we found the road ran high above steep ravines and through dark tunnels of rock, so that the sudden darkness followed rapidly by blinding sunshine played tricks with our eyesight, making driving quite hazardous. It was very beautiful, of course, with glimpses of little towns nestling far below in coves on the Mediterranean coastline, but we were relieved when at last we reached our destination just as the sun was setting.

Trepalle was indeed a small village, where everybody knew the 'Inglese' who owned the vineyard and the caravan. We collected the key from the local Bar as Lindsay had instructed, and the owner offered his son, a youth on a bicycle, to lead us to where the caravan was situated.

Dark clouds had gathered and heavy raindrops were beginning to fall as I thanked the boy, opened the gate while Richard drove through the gateway and along the track through an orchard towards the caravan. Richard unlocked the caravan door and as the heavens opened, the girls and I bolted inside, all of us laughing hysterically as the rain battered the roof of the caravan in a loud thrumming downpour. What a noisy welcome!

I towelled the girls' wet hair and when the rain eased off a little, Richard fetched our suitcases and boxes of food from the car. Soon the girls were changed out of their damp clothes and, dressed in pyjamas, they had a quick meal and were tucked up in bed, not long after followed by ourselves. It had been a long drive from Aix, and we were all exhausted.

Next morning, we ventured out into a steamy humid jungle, full of birdsong and the sound of trickling water. The heavy rain of the night before had turned the earth into a quagmire of red mud underfoot as we made our way through the vivid greens of the foliage and red poppies which grew everywhere in the brilliant sunshine. We found the vineyard, obviously well tended, with new growth of startlingly green leaves breaking out all over the gnarled black wooden stumps. Richard and I remembered that wonderful wine that we had shared with Lindsay and Bunky, and we wondered if we could find any bottles in the local shops. We went down a steep slope into a little valley where ponds had formed after the heavy rain, and where we set up a makeshift tent in a clearing. There were cliffs of red earth all around, suggesting that this might once have been a bauxite quarry.

The atmosphere in Trepalle was dominated by the constant tolling of the bells of the Catholic Church, a huge building which seemed disproportionately large for the size of the village. We met the local priest pedalling his bicycle through the main street, at the same time ringing a handbell, calling the faithful to church. In musical Italian he enquired after Lindsay's Aunt, the 'Senora Inglese'. We told him she was 'buena', and that the village was 'bellissima', which made him laugh merrily, probably at our pathetic attempts at speaking Italian. He was pleased when we told him of our plans to visit Florence and Pisa, next day and recommended several aspects of the Cathedral and Baptistry in Pisa, or at least that is what we guessed he was saying.

It was a blistering hot day when we found ourselves looking up at the famous leaning tower of Pisa. We had to climb up the tower, of course, and looked out over the panorama of the city from the slanting balcony. Later we went to the Baptistry and were walking around marvelling at the symmetry of the dome and columns of the interior when Alison suddenly decided she wanted to go to the loo. We hurried outside and enquired the way to the nearest toilets. They were miles away and Alison was obviously not going to reach them in time. We looked around us in desperation. There we were in one of the most famous places in the world, surrounded by fabulous buildings. The immaculately paved area around the Tower and Baptistry seemed to stretch forever, without a blade of grass, a bush or tree behind which our awkward infant could commune with nature. What were we to do? While we dithered, Alison wet her knickers. Well, there was no arguing with that. Who could blame her and at least it solved the immediate problem. I mopped her up, disposed of the offending garment and we made our way to the car and drove back to Trepalle. We had had quite enough for one day.

The next day we went to Florence. Taking care to locate the toilets before setting out, I led my little family on a tour of the Cathedrals, the Palazzos and the Michelangelo statues in the Piaza della Signorini. We walked over the Ponte Vecchio, which we found so crowded that we had to hold on tightly to our children, fearful of losing them in the crush.

At one end of the bridge a black African trader was crouching on the pavement behind a spread blanket covered with carved wooden figures and animals and golden trinkets, selling his wares to the passing crowd, when suddenly the police arrived. In an effort to escape, the African quickly rolled up his wares in their blanket and made a frantic dash away through the crowd. In the meleé, a woman was knocked over and hit her head on the pavement. We looked on in horror as she lay there, her husband holding her hand and calling her name. For a moment it seemed she might be dead, but then she moved, groaned and seemed to revive. We found ourselves pushed on and away from that sudden scene of violence. It had all happened so quickly that it seemed unreal, but it made me shudder to realise how easily it might have happened to one of us.

A little farther on was the world-famed Uffizi Gallery, which I insisted we should not miss. I was wrong, of course. We should have left the Uffizi for another day – another year – when the children were much older. While we stood awe-struck in front of Botticellis and Titians, Katharine and Alison, already worn out before we reached the Gallery, were getting bored. They diverted themselves by running up and down the long galleries. When we called to them Katharine stopped and came unwillingly to join us, and we hurried after the retreating little figure of

Alison to see her being picked up by a uniformed Gallery attendant and placed on a huge carved ebony chair at the end of the gallery. She sat there, too scared to move, until we came to her rescue. The attendant smiled at her and offered her a sweet as a peace offering, but she backed away and we took our leave of this long-suffering but friendly attendant and, giving up the struggle to introduce them to the Great Masters, took our little Philistines home to bed.

When Marie and Roger heard that we were going to Tuscany, Roger had asked if we would do him a favour. The year before, he and Marie had spent some time in a town not far from Trepalle where as a student in a nearby University he had produced a paper on Cardinal Newman. The paper and all his notes and books were packed in a suitcase, awaiting his return one day to collect them from the house where he and Marie had lodged. Could we please go there and collect them for him?

'Of course!' we had said. 'Pas de probleme.'

No problem. Huh! That was before we reached Trepalle and realised how deep in the Tuscan countryside their village actually was. For us now it was a day's journey there and back, through winding hilly roads and leafy lanes to a small village where we tried to locate the house where Roger and Marie had lived. At length we found someone who seemed to recognize the strange French names and knew the house. He jumped into the car and directed us, in a torrent of indecipherable but musical Italian accompanied fortunately by hand gestures, along narrow roads to a lovely old house hidden in trees a few kilometres outside the village.

There we found an old couple who remembered their lodgers, Marie and Roger and who, after we had with some difficulty explained our mission, went into the house and produced the suitcase with Roger's name printed on it. They offered us a glass of wine and we tried to answer their questions about our friends. When we explained, partly in sign language, indicating Marie's bump in the usual way, the good news that Marie was pregnant, the old lady began to count out the months on the fingers of her two gnarled old hands, finally looking up bright eyed and triumphant at her husband and our guide. We understood from what followed that the couple had not been married at the time they had lived in Italy. Oh dear! We hadn't thought of this previously, or we might have kept the information to ourselves.

The old lady obviously relished this little bit of gossip about the French couple who had been living right there in her house less than nine months ago. We left her, with her imagination and her tongue working overtime, to her moment of glory, looking forward to spreading the scandal all around the village.

As we drove away we had to laugh at the universal nature of petty gossip. That old lady was no different from women we knew in our village in Yorkshire, in Ireland and everywhere else, to whom other people's private business was of supreme interest. We had seen in the faces of gossips in those places too the same relish in counting off the months to establish whether a child was conceived before or after the marriage vows were taken. Times and customs may change but human nature is indeed very predictable, wherever you are in the world.

Our brief holiday in Tuscany was suddenly over, and we locked up the caravan, handed the key in to the Bartender, said goodbye to the lovely village of Trepalle and set off on the road back home. This time we decided to take the coastal route all the way along the Italian and French Riviera as far as Frejus, where our road to Aix turned inland.

Once again we found ourselves driving through the dark tunnels of rock and then flashing into blinding sunshine alternately so that our eyes found it difficult to adjust at such speed first to the dark, then the light. Richard and I shared the driving, so that each of us had some rest from this tiring pattern and could appreciate the magnificent scenery along that famous Riviera coastline. Most of the way we were locked into the traffic with the same car in front and another staying behind us nearly all the way to Nice. In two-way traffic on that narrow coastal road there was no alternative, although the French driver in front of us amused himself by continually passing and being passed by the driver of the car in front of him, another Frenchman. It seemed a pointless and at times dangerous exercise to us, but I suppose it was one way of staying awake and keeping boredom at bay.

CHAPTER SEVENTEEN

RETURN TO CAMPING CÉZANNE

Back in Camping Cezanne it was summer, we were gyp-
sies again, and happy to be back with our old student
friends who had struggled through a severe winter on the
campsite.

We found the Dubois family in a turmoil. There was to
be a wedding in the family. One of the older sons of this
large Catholic family was to marry in a few weeks' time
and Madame Dubois told us that she had to prepare her
house for the many guests who were expected. She was so
pleased that we were back. She wanted to ask a great
favour. Would I mind helping her in her preparation of
some of the bedrooms for the wedding guests. Would
I help her polish the furniture perhaps and clean the windows. She realised that I was not a servant, but had I not
looked after the great house Beaux Arbres so beautifully?

I wasn't so sure about that. Neither did I really want to
go from looking after one large house, to becoming the
'help' in another, but as it was a one-off situation, and in
the circumstances it was difficult to refuse Madame
Dubois, I agreed to help her prepare the house for the
happy occasion

So there I was one afternoon dressed in shorts and T-
shirt, standing on the window-sill in one of these bedrooms, cleaning the tall window, when in walked the
youngest son, Henri, a boy of about 16, to whom Richard
had been giving English lessons. I looked down at him,
suddenly realising that this room, the walls of which were
covered with posters of scantily clad female film stars and
pop singers, belonged to Henri, who was staring up at me
in a way that made me uncomfortably aware of how bare
my legs were, and how short my shorts.

I quickly finished polishing the window and made my

escape, but ever after that incident Henri became my shadow. He haunted me, broodily staring at me from the other side of the swimming pool as I lay in the sun talking to friends or playing with the children. He watched me from behind a tree, or a nearby building or tent, suddenly appearing in front of me when I was on my way to or from the shops.

Richard and our other friends noticed, of course, and teased me about my 'conquest' or laughingly accused me of 'baby snatching'. They said I should be flattered to have such a young man obviously besotted with me. But to me it had ceased to be a joke. He was stalking me, and it was not a nice feeling, especially as I couldn't get away from him. Nor could I do anything about it. I couldn't really complain to his parents on whose land we were living, and who idolised their beautiful youngest son.

Then one weekend Richard went walking in the mountains with his climbing friend Hugo from the University. He would only be away overnight and he knew that I was quite happy to stay with the children in the caravan.

We had made friends with a Dutch couple, Ingrid and Theo and their three children, who earlier had passed through Camping Cézanne on their way to the Mediterranean beaches. However, finding it too crowded and noisy there, they had returned to the serenity and beauty of Aix, where they had decided to stay for the remainder of their month's holiday. That Saturday the girls and I had just spent the whole afternoon by the pool with them and their children, and returned at supper time to our caravan to find a note pinned to the door.

In spidery handwriting it said: 'I most speak with you. Meet me tonight at midnight by the toilettes.'

At first I found this amusing. 'How romantic!!' I laughed, thinking of Henri waiting for me under the lights by the toilets.

'What does the note say, Mummy?' asked Katharine. 'Who is it from?'

Who indeed? Maybe it wasn't Henri who had written the

note. Suddenly I realised how vulnerable we were without Richard in our caravan and for the first time I felt afraid. Maybe it was someone else, more ominous. Even if it was Henri that made me feel uncomfortable. What would he do when I didn't arrive at the rendezvous?

I became so worried that I decided to go and ask Ingrid and Theo for advice. On the way to their tent the girls kept up a barrage of questions. By now they were dying to know exactly what was in the note.

Theo and Ingrid were in no doubt that the note was from Henri, and they rocked with laughter at the spelling mistakes and the ludicrous situation. They begged me to go and meet the lovesick teenager, just for the fun of it. Theo promised to follow close by, just in case things got out of hand. They chuckled again at the picture this conjured up in their imaginations, but then they sobered up when they realised that I wasn't laughing.

'I certainly will not go to meet Henri or anyone else', I protested. 'I will not leave the caravan.'

'Don't worry, Janie. We will protect you,' said Ingrid, giving me a reassuring hug. In the end it was decided that Theo should go to the rendezvous at midnight just to check that it was Henri who was waiting there and not someone else.

I put the children to bed that night as late as I could at about ten o'clock, when Theo and Ingrid came over to the caravan to keep me company as they knew I was annoyed and more than a little scared by the whole situation. We talked through the evening and finished off two or three bottles of wine 'to give us Dutch courage', joked Theo. At midnight Theo went out to the Rendezvous. Ingrid stayed with me, obviously finding the situation very exciting.

At length Theo returned, confirming that Henri had indeed been waiting under the light by the toilettes. After talking to him for some time, and telling him that he was very wrong to take advantage of Richard's absence to make such an approach to me, Theo had told Henri to go home because I would not be coming to meet him.

When Richard returned, Theo and Ingrid told him all about the weekend's exciting events. Richard was amused at first, but at the same time he was rather annoyed at Henri's behaviour. He realised how threatened I had felt and he was grateful that I had been able to turn to Theo and Ingrid for help. We both were.

Richard decided it was time to have a word with young Henri. While he felt a bit sorry for the young man, remembering what it was like to be a lovesick teenager, this time Henri had gone too far.

The next morning, Richard went to see Henri, making it very clear to the teenager that he was making a nuisance of himself, that I was getting very annoyed and that the affair of the note was the last straw. It had to stop or we would be forced to make a formal complaint to Monsieur and Madame Dubois. Henri was embarrassed, but he took the hint and stopped stalking me.

When we returned to Aix years later with the girls, by now teenagers themselves, we went to Camping Cezanne to look up our old friends the Dubois family. Monsieur and Madame Dubois were still there, much older, of course. The children of the Dubois family were all grown up and married. Some of Henri's many brothers were still there with their wives, helping to run the campsite but, they told us proudly, Henri was now living in Paris where he was a well known poet and pop singer.

The girls were impressed. A pop singer! I was very impressed, Henri – a poet!

CHAPTER EIGHTEEN

OUR DUTCH FRIENDS

Theo and Ingrid became firm friends. Their two boys, Bartolomeo and Rudy, and their daughter Marianne, although older than Katharine, played with our two little girls who adored all three children.

We spent long days by the pool where the Dutch boys tirelessly leapt about, diving noisily into the water with two Portuguese youths who had just arrived with their parents. Marianne was quieter and she and Katharine swam in the shallow end, while Alison, still unable to swim, sat by the steel ladder, dipping a cautious toe in the water, watching the others enviously.

One day I looked around to check that the children were all happy, and I realised that Alison had disappeared. I looked everywhere, in the pool, around the side, where the others were playing, but there was no sign of her. Had they seen her? Yes, she had been with them just now, but no one seemed to have seen her go away and no one had any idea where she might be.

Suddenly the happy afternoon clouded over. Richard and I, now thoroughly alarmed, started to hunt in all the places where we thought she might have gone. We went to the caravan but she wasn't there. We tried the swings, but again there was no Alison. We went to the Restaurant, to the toilets, to the Happy Lion, drawing a blank every time. After trying all her favourite haunts, we approached the awful place we didn't want to think of but which had been in the back of our minds all along.

It was a large pond, nearly a lake, full of muddy water, full of weeds, where we sometimes went boating with the children. Surely she wouldn't have gone into that murky water, not Alison, who wasn't all that keen on getting wet, even in the shallow end of the swimming pool. So I reasoned to myself, conscious all the time that we were running out of alternatives, and aware that Richard was organising a search party to explore the weedy margins of the pond. I couldn't bear it and hastened back to the caravan, one more time, hoping against hope that whatever was wrong, Alison would always head for home. How overwhelmed with happiness and relief I felt when I saw the little blond haired figure walking up the path from the caravan towards me.

I ran towards her, picked her up and hugged her, crying with relief.

'What's the matter, Mummy?' she asked, her little arms hugging tightly round my neck.

'We couldn't find you, darling,' I sobbed. 'We thought you were...' and then, remembering the search we had made of the entire campsite, I asked. 'Where were you, Alison?'

'At the caravan, Mummy. I needed my potty. ' Alison was on the edge of tears, realising how upset I was. 'I -I'm sorry.'

'It's all right Darling. You're safe. That's all that matters.' I hugged her again, tears rolling down my cheeks. Then I remembered the search that was still going on.

'We must go up to the pond and tell Daddy and Katharine and the others. They're all looking for you.'

Alison looked bewildered and a bit scared. It was beginning to dawn on her that she had caused a lot of trouble. I carried her in my arms but she was too heavy for me on that steep upward slope and soon I had to put her down. Hand in hand we hurried to the pond.

Richard saw us from a distance and came running towards us, tears of relief in his eyes, and Katharine was running behind him, shouting 'Alison! Alison! ' When they reached us there were hugs and kisses all round.

The awful search was called off. Everyone shared in our joy at finding Alison, and worried faces turned to smiles and laughter as our friends realised the emergency was over. Alison had survived yet again.

She was the centre of attention and was beginning to enjoy her moment of celebrity. We took her back to the caravan, and although we were overcome with relief and just wanted to hold her close, of course we had to tell her how worried we had been, how much trouble everyone had been to, and that she must promise never, ever to go off on her own again like that without any warning.

'I promise,' said Alison, and she really meant it.

To celebrate, the Dutch family came with us the following weekend to that wonderful beach we had glimpsed all those months ago at St. Marie de la Mer, on our way to the Becker's house for lunch. It was a glorious day. The sun shone all day long, and this time, unlike our previous visit, there was no Mistral to whip up the sand in our faces. The white sandy beach stretched in an unbroken line from East to West as far as the eye could see, a free and limitless playground for the children who, after swimming, threw off their wet clothes, ran races, made sandcastles, played with beach balls, collected seashells and splashed in and out of the sapphire sea all the perfect day long.

At midday we called everyone together for our picnic, and afterwards, while the men took the children along the beach for a walk and a game of football, Ingrid and I had a siesta. Later, while the children returned to their play, Theo and Ingrid, Richard and I basked in the sun on the white beach, talked and slept the afternoon away. It was a rare and shining day, full of warmth and brilliant colour and good company, never to be forgotten.

We kept in touch with Theo and Ingrid and their family in Rotterdam for many years afterwards. Over the years we have often thought how easy it was throughout that year to make friends, lasting friends, and one reason I am sure was that because we did not live in a house, people felt free to visit us in our caravan and come in and join us. There were no walls to keep them out and the door was open more often than not, especially in the wonderful summer heat of Provence, where living out of doors seemed natural and therefore meeting other people was so informal and easy.

More and more holiday makers were coming through on their way South to the coast and we watched from our caravan home as campers arrived, usually late in the afternoon or early evening, tired from a long day on the Autoroute, and proceeded to put up a frame tent that they had probably not seen for twelve months. We saw marriages totter, as nerves clanged like the hopeless confusion of pieces of metal which were thrown to the ground when they would not link up. When, frustrating hours later, the tent was finally up, the family were often too tired to do more than have a quick bite to eat and fall into bed.

But next day the serious business of camping would begin. The kitchen tent, complete with every modern camping convenience, would take shape while in the main family tent the television had pride of place so that while Madame took her accustomed place in the kitchen cooking elaborate meals for her family, Monsieur would settle down to watch the evening news – and all his other favourite programmes.

We felt vastly superior to these 'couch potatoes' who were slumped in front of a television set night after night in their tents and caravans. The thought of taking a television set on a camping holiday in Provence seemed to us a travesty.

Apart from the two weeks when we had acted as house sitters for Janet and Jean-Marc we had seen no television for nearly a year. There had been no television set at Beaux Arbres. We were making the most of a long holiday from the tyranny of television, so hard to resist at home, but here we had never missed it. We were out of doors most of the day, and when the darkness sent us back to the caravan the children went to bed, Richard had his studies, while for me there was always another great book to read or the English Sunday newspaper which we bought in France on Mondays. That alone kept me reading for hours.

CHAPTER NINETEEN

LA CUISINE FRANCAISE

We never ceased to be amazed at the time French women spent cooking on a campsite. They never stopped being housewives, apparently bringing all the household chores with them, and scorning all the short cuts that other European women took on holiday. We would see them go shopping in the morning, coming back laden with groceries. Preparation and cooking of lunch would fill the rest of the morning. The other members of the family would appear for lunch at midday or thereabouts, and the meal would stretch into the afternoon. Then while the family disappeared once more, the mother would wash up. After a brief interval, when she probably had a siesta, she would emerge again, and begin to the lengthy preparation of the evening meal. At six or seven o'clock the family would convene for this important ritual which lasted until the children's bedtime. Then the television would go on, and Madame would once again begin clearing up.

One day I was feeling rather ill after having been on the beach in hot sunshine all morning and afternoon at Carry le Rouet. My skin was reddening and I had obviously had a touch of sunstroke. Richard told me to lie down and take it easy while he would look after the evening meal. I wasn't feeling much like cooking or eating and gratefully retired to my bed. Meantime, Richard and the girls hailed the Pizza Van, which toured the campsite each evening. Returning to the caravan with the hot pizza, Richard served it up to the girls and himself with plenty of salad and some crisp fresh bread and butter. They wasted no time eating this delicious instant meal, and after a quick drink of orange juice the three went out again about fifteen minutes later, heading for the ice-cream shop in Val

St. André for an instant dessert.

Unknown to us, all this had been witnessed by the lady in a neighbouring tent, who was busily preparing vegetables for the evening meal. Incredulous, she asked Richard if he and the girls had eaten in the brief time since she had seen them enter the caravan with the Pizza.

'Oh Yes!' said Richard happily. 'We had a lovely meal. We're off out now.'

'Oh! La La! Les Anglais!' exclaimed the French lady in pitying astonishment and hastened back into the tent to tell the rest of her family about our Philistine eating habits.

I asked this dedicated cook-housewife if she ever had a holiday from cooking. She was most affronted. Never, she declared, would a French woman allow her family to go without a decent meal, as women of other nationalities appeared happy to do. (This with a pointed look in my direction).

I do admire the dedication of such selfless wives and mothers, but I thank heaven that I was not destined to spend my life in the kitchen. Everyone needs a day off, now and again, especially on holiday, even the cook!

In any case, at that time in France it was possible to find an excellent meal in a good restaurant at very little cost. This provided us with an enjoyable weekly night out on the town which we felt we needed, even in our impoverished student year in France. We couldn't really afford it, I suppose, but we enjoyed the French food enormously and although the reckoning was to come later, we did not regret this minor extravagance.

I remember some wonderful evenings, sitting with friends around a table in a local bistro, enjoying the warmth, the delicious food, the mingling aromas of garlic and herbs coming from the kitchen and more often than not, the music of some wandering minstrel, who might have been a student 'moonlighting' to support his studies. It was all part of the heady atmosphere, which made that year so rich and memorable.

One evening we went with friends to a little restaurant

crammed with noisy diners and found a place at one of the tables overflowing outside on to the pavement. We studied the two set menus, the equivalent in Francs of about ten pounds and twenty pounds. Predictably, we all chose the former, though even that was an indulgence. The waitress was petite, not much taller than we were, seated at the table. She was very busy that evening as every table was taken. She came, almost running, laden with course after course, beginning with a huge 'plateau' heaped high with oysters, which were almost too much for us, but we somehow managed to finish them. The succeeding courses were equally generous, and of superb quality. The Restaurant had been highly recommended by a friend and we had been told to expect a great meal, but even so, we were astonished and delighted to eat so incredibly well for the relatively small cost.

As we pushed away our coffee cups at the end of the meal, amid sighs of contentment, we called to the little waitress for our bill. This was the moment of truth. Each couple produced their twenty pounds plus their half share of the cost of wine and tips. The bill, however, was for just less than a hundred pounds. We looked at each other, first in amazement, then in horror. We had obviously eaten the more expensive meal. No wonder it had been so generous, so altogether 'formidable'.

Richard was rolling up his shirt-sleeves. 'A la vaisselles, mes camarades! ' he declared, pushing his chair away and standing up.

Now it was the turn of the waitress to look surprised. Richard explained that we had ordered the less expensive meal. At first her eyes registered confusion, then distress, as she checked her notebook and accepted that this was indeed the truth.

'Moment, M'sieurs, Dames,' she begged, hurrying away. A few minutes later she returned with the manager, who quickly acknowledged that a mistake had been made, for which the fault was certainly not ours. We would be charged for the meal we had ordered.

When we enquired about the fate of the waitress, the manager assured us that no blame would be attached to her. It was a genuine mistake, on a very busy evening. He hoped we had enjoyed our meal and would come again.

There was no problem about that. We certainly would, we assured him. And as often as we could afford it, we certainly did return to that Restaurant, and every time we were welcomed as valued customers, and were given a wonderful meal, but we always made sure that our waitress understood which meal we wanted.

CHAPTER TWENTY

AU CINÉMA

Apart from our weekly nights out at a Restaurant we sometimes went to the cinema. Although mostly we saw French films and many of those were most enjoyable, we occasionally were glad to see an English or American film, with English dialogue, usually with French subtitles. It was certainly more enjoyable for me not to have to translate all through a film.

One night we went to see 'Le Messager', with Julie Christie and Alan Bates in the starring roles, and with French sub-titles. It soon became obvious that we were the only members of the audience who were able to follow the English dialogue, because we stood out as the only ones who laughed.

It is a sombre tale, based on the novel 'The Go-Between' by L. P. Hartley, which we had read, but there are brighter moments in it, especially in the light-hearted banter between the two schoolboys, and we laughed merrily while the rest of the audience worked hard reading the subtitles, finding little there to amuse them. Heads turned when yet again we fell about laughing at some ridiculous situation or remark. The French audience simply couldn't imagine what we found so funny, and of course that made us laugh even more.

About half way through the summer term there was a great furore about a French film that was being shown at a local cinema. The film was based on the true story of an ill-fated love affair, which had flared a few years ago between a teenage schoolboy and a young female teacher at one of the Lycées in Aix.

The cinema had quickly realised that this was a local box office winner, and had increased the cost of tickets accordingly, much to the disgust of our French student friends, who nevertheless queued with the crowds of local people to see this film. Our friends then told us all about the plot but urged that we must see the film for ourselves, as it revealed much that was wrong with so-called French morality.

Eventually we saw the film, a tragic tale of a liaison between a handsome boy aged about seventeen and a young female teacher who was only about five or six years older than him. The relative ages of the lovers seemed less important than the fact that the boy was a pupil and seen as a victim while the young woman was a teacher, however young. Because she was considered to have abused the trust placed in her, she was held responsible and dismissed from her post.

When the two lovers ran away together, the hunt was on, with the Police and the press pursuing them like hounds. When, inevitably, they were found together, in a hotel somewhere on the Riviera, the boy was 'rescued' by his family and the young teacher was arrested and imprisoned, pending trial.

As the case had aroused national interest, the media made the most of this 'cause célebre', allowing no detail of the teacher's life to remain untouched. The love affair between this young woman and the teenage boy, a genuine affair of the heart, was painted in lurid colours. She was portrayed as a child abuser, her character totally destroyed in the process. Unable to bear the thought of the trial, and the disgrace that she had brought upon herself and her family, the young woman committed suicide in the prison.

The fact that the tragedy had begun in one of the schools in Aix made it all the more riveting, and the film was a source of heated discussion and argument among the students, whose sympathy was almost completely with the woman.

What after all was her crime? She had hurt no-one. She had merely fallen in love. To many of those young French people the real villains of the piece were the press, who had hounded her to her death.

It was indeed a tragic story and we were strangely affected by it, but even so, we were astonished at the passionate response of the French public and the depth to which the students identified with this 'crime passionel' until we heard that there were rumours circulating at the University about a similar affair between a young and attractive female lecturer in the Geography Department and one of the male students. When the University Principal heard of this affair the lecturer had been reprimanded by her Head of Department, and was under threat of dismissal.

When details of the story got out, the students showed their support for the female lecturer by turning up in droves at her lectures. This was all the more remarkable in that revolutionary year when many lectures were interrupted by left wing students who would forcibly close down a lecture given by an unpopular lecturer if he or she did not reflect their political views. On other occasions they would infiltrate lecture halls, barracking the lecturers, and making it impossible for the lecture to be heard.

It was indeed a strange coincidence that the film about the teacher who had committed suicide in a similar situation should come to the cinema in Aix at that time, and it was certainly not lost on the student population, who flocked to see the controversial film.

Towards the end of the summer term there was an exciting occasion when the Aix Festival staged the Mozart Opera, Don Giovanni in the open air in the Cours Mirabeau. With some friends we dressed up grandly and, oblivious of the hard seats, we were transported through a long hot evening by Mozart's glorious music. The trees and statues and buildings of our beloved Cours Mirabeau surrounded us, but for once we were almost unaware of them – until that is, the statue of Faust's father suddenly came to life. There was a gasp from the audience. I felt my hair stand on end, my skin freeze. It was a truly terrifying moment. We had all accepted the statue at one side of the street as a stone statue, and then it moved, it spoke, and in a deep baritone it intoned Faust's terrible fate. I never experienced such an awesome moment in any theatre and I'll never forget that moment of drama as long as I live.

CHAPTER TWENTY-ONE

CHEZ SYLVIE

For some time we had known a young Frenchwoman who liked to practice speaking English with us. We had met her at someone's party, and kept bumping into her at the supermarché, where she would inevitably say 'You must come round for a meal sometime.' This was, we thought, just one of those empty invitations that some people feel it necessary to make, with no intention of ever following them up.

In Sylvie's case we were wrong. One hot Saturday morning Richard was sitting in the caravan talking to a Welshman whom he had met in the University. Gavin, who was a very argumentative character, had turned up unexpectedly. I was busy putting together a picnic lunch for a family day out at Carry le Rouet, and I groaned inwardly, thinking that if Gavin didn't go soon Richard would ask him to come with us. Gavin was not the sort of person in whose company one could relax on the beach – or anywhere else. Our open door policy sometimes had its drawbacks, I was thinking ruefully when a head popped round the door.

'Hullo! Can I come in? ' It was Sylvie, the young French woman whom we kept meeting at the supermarché.

'I invite you to come to dinner with us this evening,' she said after introductions. It seemed rather casual and last minute to me but I could not really think of any excuse, except that we had no babysitter.

'Oh, we'll get one of the students to baby-sit', offered Richard.

'Oh, that's fine,' declared Sylvie, 'We'll expect you at nine. Oh, and bring your friend.'

'Who? Me?' Gavin was grinning with delight at this unexpected invitation'. 'Gee, thanks, Sylvie. I'd love to come.'

'Well, Gee,' I said later to Richard on the way to the beach, 'It was a long time in coming, but now that she has actually invited us, I don't really want to go, especially not with Gavin. He bores me to tears.'

Richard laughed. 'I could see you trying to wriggle out of it, but between Sylvie and Gavin you didn't have a chance, did you?

We dashed back early from the beach, collected Ingrid, the Swedish girl student who was our regular baby sitter, and after a hurried shower we got ourselves ready for the unexpected dinner party. Gavin was already there when we arrived just after nine, and we could hear his voice even before the door opened. Sylvie welcomed us like long lost friends, and introduced us to her husband, Claude, a rather miserable looking young man.

While Gavin carried on a lively conversation with Sylvie in the kitchen, Claude poured us a drink. He asked us if we would like to see the children, and we followed him into a bedroom where two little boys were sleeping in bunk beds with brightly coloured duvets tucked around them.

Suddenly Claude burst into tears, and turned to us, saying 'Do you realise that Sylvie is leaving me?' We shook our heads dumbly. 'Tomorrow morning she is going away – with a Catholic priest from the Seychelles.'

We looked at him aghast. He surely couldn't be making it up. It was so unlikely that it must be true. He assured us that it was. They had been on holiday in the Seychelles when Sylvie had met the said Priest and the two had fallen in love and had a torrid affair. Claude had hoped it would fade away when the holiday came to an end, but apparently it had not, and now he was being abandoned in favour of a defrocked priest.

'What about the children?' I asked.

'She's taking them with her,' replied Claude, and once again burst out crying.

Just then Sylvie called us to the dinner table and there followed one of the most bizarre evenings of my experience. I couldn't take part in the conversation, which was carried on mostly between Sylvie and a sparkling Gavin. Claude was speechless too, and Richard said very little. We could hardly swallow the food that Sylvie put in front of us.

We were actually glad that Gavin was there. He was the star of the show, chattering gaily away to Sylvie, who looked remarkably calm for someone who was going through such a traumatic episode in her life.

We came to the conclusion afterwards that Sylvie had deliberately invited us so that she would not have to speak to her husband on their last evening together in the same house. Richard and I, and more effectively Gavin, acted as a buffer between the two warring parties that evening. I felt profoundly sorry for poor Claude and I hoped he would not do anything desperate that night to himself or to his unfaithful wife. Obviously he didn't because we bumped into him the next day at the supermarché and although he looked pretty miserable, he seemed to have accepted the situation. He told us that his wife had got up early that morning, packed up her bags and the children, driven off with her priest and left her husband without a backward look.

Poor Claude. I wish we could have done something to help, but we hardly knew him and in any case we were feeling pretty miserable ourselves. We were coming to the end of our final term at the University and would very soon have to pack up and go home to England.

Chapter Twenty-Two

END OF TERM

The attitude of the Dubois family changed noticeably as their campsite filled up with tents and caravans. Suddenly we were regarded with a cooler eye. We were taking up too much space. We were paying too little. Our rentals had been arranged on a long-term basis, but this arrangement no longer applied now that the summer camping season had arrived. Summer rates were high, far too high for us in our impoverished state.

We no longer felt that we were welcome guests, even privileged friends of the family, as we had done before. Monsieur Dubois, his wife, his sons, were too busy running the office, the restaurant, the swimming pool and all the numerous tasks involved in organising a large popular campsite. We understood, we certainly didn't blame them, but felt rather excluded from all the activity which left us on the fringes of life in Cézanne. We had to wake up as from a dream and face the fact that it was time to pack up our bags and go home.

We went around our old haunts one last time. Everywhere we went things seemed to be changing beyond recognition. Our favourite restaurants had taken on new staff and even the old familiar staff were usually too busy to have time to talk to us. The clientele had changed too. The holiday crowds were moving in to the hotels, the restaurants and the pavement cafés. When we went for one last time to Carry le Rouet, we found the little beach covered with bronzing bodies, the small car park noisy and dusty with more and more people arriving on holiday. We didn't even try to go near the Riviera.

Many of our friends including the English students from York had gone home for the summer while others had found jobs somewhere in the region. We heard from Ros that she had a summer job in a hotel in Aix, where she cleaned twenty-eight baths every morning!

Richard had been offered a job in a college teaching English as a foreign language. He had already done some tutoring in this college earlier in the summer term when they asked him to come in to give their students practice in English conversation just before their final examinations. For this he had been paid the equivalent of forty pounds per day, which to us seemed fantastic. However, the salary offered for the summer course was rather less and we thought we would find it difficult to survive on it.

On the other hand, while we had no idea what we would do when we returned to England, Richard felt sure he would find a job and at least we would be able to move into our own house again. With the ending of the academic year our tenant, the Professor, had finished his work in York and was on his way home to Canada. We were grateful to this man who had had paid our mortgage each month during our absence but now we would have to find the money for this commitment ourselves. We faced the fact that we couldn't afford to stay on in France, with our sizeable overdraft increasing by the day. The sooner we were on our way home the better.

I told myself that I had at least something to look forward to. Having spent so much time with the students over the past year, I had decided that I would apply to the Open University, which had just completed its first year. Everything I had read in the English Sunday papers about this new project had been impressive, and from France I had sent in an application to the Open University and been accepted as an arts student in the year beginning the following January. I was thrilled that the opportunity to study, which had so long eluded me, was now a reality and the fact that I could do the course from home meant that I could avoid the problems and costs of leaving my children with childminders.

Richard, however, was far from enthusiastic at the prospect of returning to York. The dreaded interview with our Bank Manager awaited him and he was only too well aware of how much money we owed the Bank, with no immediate prospect of paying off the overdraft. 'Live now, pay later' had been our motto for most of the time we had been in France, and at the time it had seemed well worth the financial risk. Now the day of reckoning was almost upon us and it was scary.

We made the rounds of all our favourite places in Aix, and were invited to farewell meals and parties at the houses of our many friends. We bid them 'Au Revoir' promising to return to Aix soon, but all the time with a sinking feeling in our hearts in the knowledge that we were coming to the end of our wonderful adventure.

On the last afternoon we went to Vauvenargues and sat with a cool drink at a pavement cafe under the tall shady trees that lined the main street of that lovely village. We had hoped to find Vauvenargues as quiet and secluded as ever, but even here the holiday crowds were moving in. Richard and I went over yet again the well-worn arguments for staying at least a little longer. But we both knew it was pointless. We looked at each other in resignation. Reluctantly we dragged ourselves back to the campsite to face the final task of packing up the caravan ready for our journey home next day.

Early next morning, before departing, we exchanged 'Au Revoirs' with the Dubois family and thanked them for their friendship. They had been very good to us and we really meant it when we promised to return one day. Then with heavy hearts, we hitched up the car to the caravan and prepared to move off. As the caravan edged away from its site a large toad was suddenly exposed to the sunlight in the space where our caravan had stood. We had no idea how long this creature might have been there, but it certainly explained why the night noises of nature in Provence had sometimes seemed very close.

I remember very little about the return journey through France, except that as we reached the autoroute, with the sun behind us and Mont St. Victoire and the hills of Provence fading in the distance, we found ourselves very much in a minority heading northwards. On the south-ward lanes, however, for kilometre after kilometre, the autoroute was a steady stream of traffic. It seemed to us that the entire population of France, and possibly much of the rest of Europe, was heading south at the beginning of the summer holiday season.

Once again we asked ourselves were we doing the right thing. Were we crazy to be going home when everyone else was happily going on holiday. The impulse to turn at the next motorway exit and join the holiday traffic south-wards was very tempting. But it was too late. We had made our decision and there was no going back. Besides, we argued, with perhaps a touch of sour grapes, it wouldn't be the same. The southbound travellers were welcome to the crowded roads and car parks and beaches – the inflat-ed prices in hotels and campsites and restaurants. They were more than welcome to the noisy overcrowded town centres and the discomfort and intense heat of the high summer.

With such reassurances we sought to persuade our-selves that it was right to be going home. After all, we had experienced Provence at its very best – its superb scenery, its incomparable light and colour, the warmth and 'joie de vivre' of the Provencale people, and so much more. It had been a marvellous experience, one that would influence the rest of our lives. As we sped our way northwards through the French countryside I could only hope that one day in the future, when we had resolved the unfin-ished business awaiting us in York, we could return to Provence, possibly never to leave again.

We had decided to use the Autoroutes on the return journey as we felt we should get home as soon as possible. Our house awaited, and we needed to find work quickly. Besides, we didn't want to prolong the agony of leaving a country that we had come to love. Best to cut the ties cleanly and quickly and get back to face the Bank Manager, earning a living and paying our debts. The dream was over.

CHAPTER TWENTY-THREE

HOME AGAIN

Back in England we experienced the culture shock of a cold wet night in Dover, and the sight of some people on the campsite eating fish and chips out of soggy paper wrappers did nothing to restore our spirits. Oh for those wonderful French Restaurants on the sunny pavements of Aix!

Next morning we set out early and reached London in bright sunshine. Our spirits lifted. We had a cunning plan which had been hatched while we were still in France. Having parked the car and caravan in the only double parking place we could find in the west end Richard paid for the two parking meters which our car and caravan required. I entered the caravan in shorts and T-shirt and emerged a few minutes later, smartly dressed for an interview I had arranged with one of the London based Secretarial Agencies whose advertisements I had studied with interest in the English Sunday papers while we were still in France. The salaries had seemed incredibly high and in the absence of any other offers, Richard had agreed that I should apply for a work as a 'temp' and try to attend an interview at a Secretarial Agency on our way through London on the journey home.

The interview was another jolt to the system, involving a test of shorthand and typing, all the most difficult and tricky spellings they could think of, and a thorough investigation of my recent, or in my case, not-so-recent experience. I returned to the caravan, shell-shocked and thoroughly pessimistic about my chances of getting a job.

The caravan was deserted, I had no key, the parking meter had run out of cash and a uniformed traffic warden was bearing down on me with a beady look in his eye, pen and penalty book at the ready. I had to think quickly.

'Look, I'm sorry but I've lost my key, my husband has gone home to get the duplicate, and meantime the meter has run out of time. Would it be all right if I put some more money in.' It sounded a highly unlikely story, even to me.

The warden looked dubious. He had heard a good many tales in his time, but this one had him scratching his head in bewilderment. I held my breath.

'Oh well, all right then,' he said at length, 'I believe you. Thousands wouldn't. But don't let it happen again,' and he moved on to his next victim.

'As if,' I thought to myself, restraining the urge to laugh out loud, but the danger was past, and I had avoided a fine we could well do without. When Richard showed up a few minutes later with the girls, I quickly briefed him, just in case the warden showed up again. A few minutes later we joined the busy city traffic, and eventually escaped the city northwards on the way home to York.

It was very late when we reached home. How strange it was to be back in our own house again, back in our own beds. But we were all too exhausted to think about it then. The girls were too sleepy to do more than crawl into bed, and Richard and I decided to leave all the unpacking until after we had a good night's sleep.

Next morning there was a telephone call from the Secretarial Agency asking me to start work the following Monday with a firm in the City of London. My initial pleasure gave way to panic when I realised what I had let myself in for. Richard too, suddenly faced with being a house-husband with two lively children to feed and look after, started to have second thoughts. However, we needed the money, and in the absence of any other work, we had no choice.

That weekend it was panic stations, with so much to arrange, and all the washing, cooking and shopping to think about for Richard and the children. Then of course I had to get ready for an indeterminate period of working in London, packing a suitcase with suitable clothes both for work and relaxing in. I had a feeling of unreality and near terror at the prospect of leaving home and facing unknown challenges, but there was little time to worry about it, only moments to say 'Hello' and 'Goodbye' to friends and neighbours, hug my family and then on Sunday evening Richard and the girls saw me off at York station on the train to London.

On the way to London I felt totally disorientated. What on earth was I doing, leaving my home and family and setting off on such a crazy scheme? I felt like getting out at the next station and taking the next train back to York. But I continued on the journey, reasoning that if it didn't make any more sense by the next weekend I would go home then.

In the absence of a better solution, I had arranged to stay at the Y.W.C.A. in Russell Square, and suddenly found myself one of the anonymous crowd of office workers surging to work in London each morning. After the initial shock, I found I quite enjoyed being an independent woman again, meeting lots of new people in the office and in the Y.W.C.A. and looking up several old friends who lived in London and nearby.

That first weekend, instead of going home, I went to visit Lindsay's family in Sussex, where I met up again with Lindsay and Bunky, who were staying with her parents for the summer holidays. Also visiting that weekend was Lindsay's Aunt Dodie who had a large house in Putney in which she offered me a spare room while I was working in London. Over the next two weeks I had a great time. I was more at home in the office, where I found my work as secretary to the managing Director of an Engineering firm much appreciated. Aunt Dodie cooked wonderful evening meals for me after work each evening except when I went to shows and plays in the West End with new friends. Suddenly my life was transformed. I felt years younger with a great job, no responsibilities, no housework, and a husband and family in York managing fine without me.

Except that they weren't. I had nightly phone calls from Richard begging me to come home. Katharine complained that she and Alison couldn't eat Richard's cooking, and consumed a lot of Cornflakes! Alison added her 'Please come home Mummy,' to the chorus from York. Then Richard found a job, as a dumper driver with the builders on the nearly finished housing estate on which we lived, and he promptly demanded that I return home to look after my children.

Reluctantly, I handed in my notice to my employer, who begged me to stay. He said I was the best Secretary he had ever had and offered me a permanent job at a fantastic salary if only I would stay. But it was not to be. A week later I was back in York, in the bosom of my family. It had been fun in London while it lasted and I had made some money for the family coffers, but the welcome I got from Richard and children made up for everything. They had really missed me. They had certainly missed my cooking, and they were very appreciative of every meal set in front of them for some time after my return.

The neighbours were pleased to see us safely home again from France, and when they enquired about my absence in London they were very concerned at our impecunious state. One of them worked at Bournville, the chocolate firm in York, and he helpfully suggested Richard might like to apply for a job that had become vacant, shovelling cocoa into a machine that made Smarties. With a straight face Richard solemnly thanked him for his concern, but decided that he preferred the outdoor life on the building site. Only the girls were disappointed, as they had been looking forward to all the free Smarties that our kind neighbour's children had told them went with the job.

Some of our neighbours told us that they had kept a friendly eye on the Canadian Professor who had been very quiet and very busy, an ideal tenant and neighbour. They had however, been concerned when one morning the curtains remained closed and stayed closed all day and for several days thereafter. They were worried that the Professor was ill or worse, dead, and were about to call in the Police when suddenly, one morning, the curtains were opened again and all returned to normal. He had simply gone away for a few days.

We ourselves found that Professor Bulmer had never used the open fire, which we had so carefully taught him to light. Instead he had bought portable oil filled radiators, which he offered to us for a reasonable price. The coal-bunker was still filled with the unused coal we had left for him, and in the sideboard were unopened bottles of whisky, gin, brandy, and several bottles of wine, which he had left for us as a generous welcome home present. The house was immaculate, everything in order. How lucky we were in our choice of tenant.

Richard told me that the Bank Manager had been quite decent about the overdraft. Although it was over two thousand pounds, a huge sum to us in those days, he knew that we had the house as security against our debt and he was impressed that we were both making such efforts to earn some money. Besides, as the manager of a Bank mostly used by students, he was familiar with our situation and could bide his time until better times ahead. He was right, of course, and two years later when we sold the house in York and moved to Edinburgh where Richard had found a job as a French teacher, we paid off the overdraft and had enough money remaining to put down as deposit on a house in our new location.

The school holidays came to an end rather quickly and suddenly Katharine started school. We found an excellent morning nursery school for Alison and the girls settled down with their friends again and appeared to forget all about life in France. They also, to our disappointment, forgot the language. We tried to keep them speaking French at home, but they no longer saw it as fun or as relevant to their lives and in time, much to their relief, we gave up the effort. In October, Richard resumed his studies at York University and life returned to something like normality.

We sold the caravan, reluctantly, to a farmer in one of the Yorkshire Dales, where we had parked it for some months after returning home, with the idea of spending weekends there. However, when the farmer's wife offered to buy it we agreed a price and went to the farm one weekend to complete the deal. The farmer's wife went upstairs to get the money and a few minutes later we heard heavy footsteps coming down the wooden staircase. She entered the room, carrying a huge, metal safe-box, which she dropped on the wooden table in front of us with a crash. We watched, fascinated, as she unlocked the box and proceeded to count out in silver 50p pieces, a couple of hundred pounds in payment for the caravan. Thanking her, we put the coins in a plastic bag, which she gave us for the purpose. Richard picked up the bag, which weighed a ton and we got up to go. But before we left the room I simply had to ask the question, which had been puzzling me.

'Why have you paid us in 50p pieces'

'We don't trust paper money,' the farmer's wife replied in her strong Yorkshire accent.

'No, nor Banks neither', added her husband darkly from the fireside chair.

We made a hasty exit and managed to reach the car, out of earshot of the good farmer and his wife, before bursting into gales of laughter.

'Well, it just goes to show you', said Richard, exactly mimicking the broad vowels of his native Yorkshire. 'There's nowt so queer as folks.'

Now we knew we were home again.

The autumn passed quickly and I was soon immersed in my studies with the Open University. I attended weekly seminars, frequent lectures at York University, and my life filled up with writing assignments and reading course units and books, which I somehow had to fit in between all the multiple tasks and responsibilities of running a home and a family.

Provence seemed far off, both in time and space, and I hated to think that soon we would retain only vague memories of all the fun we had in the caravan, and those incredible months we spent in Beaux Arbres. However, as we looked at the photographs of our happy daughters and recalled the many friends we had made and places we had loved in Provence, the colours seemed no less vivid, the details only a little less sharp as time went by.

Our experiences in Provence had been so rich, in spite of the fact that we had never been so poor in financial terms. Those days in the sun in the last year we had the girls all to ourselves before their schooldays suddenly seemed so precious to me that I was determined they should not fade away as so many other days had faded. But how could I prevent the process of forgetfulness? I knew that Alison would probably remember nothing of Provence. Katharine might remember some details but she too would forget most of the experience. So I made a promise to my daughters. 'I'll write it all down for you,' I said. 'One day maybe I'll write a book!'

Now, many years later, when my little girls are young women, I have kept my promise.

LE RETOUR